Learn at Your Own Risk:
9 Strategies for Thriving in a Pandemic and Beyond

by

Tom Haymes

Learn at Your Own Risk:
9 Strategies for Thriving in a Pandemic and Beyond
by
Tom Haymes

ISBN – 9781626133013
LCCN – 2020949373

Copyright 2020

Published by ATBOSH Media ltd.

Cleveland, Ohio, USA
http://www.ATBOSH.com

Some of the materials in this book were adapted from Tom Haymes' work previously published on eCampusNews, Current Issues in Education (the STAC Model chapter), and ideaspaces.net.
All rights were retained by the author.

Table of Contents

Foreword 1
Exiting the Pandemic:
A Model for Education Going Forward

Introduction 7
A Crisis Design Primer for Teachers

PART I
Overcoming Transactional Teaching Using Tools and Transparency

Chapter 1 21
Use Tasks to Drive Your Toolsets
- Teaching should drive technology
- A strategy for pairing technology with teaching

Chapter 2 43
Listening and Learning in an Era of Social Distancing
- Learning is fundamentally conversational
- Nurturing conversations is the key to navigate shifts in technology and circumstance

Chapter 3 59
The Currency of Teaching
- Education has become transactional
- Changing assessment strategies is critical in transcending this barrier to learning

PART II
Teaching and Learning Holistically to Harness Time and Space

Chapter 4 73
Creating Informal Spaces to Support Atomized Learning
- Most learning happens outside the classroom
- The STAC Model is a set of design principles to nurture and support informal learning, both online and in-person

Chapter 5 97
Tuning Instruction for a Digital World
- Digital gives us the opportunity to reimagine what a course looks like
- See what a 2-year redesign process looks like as of today

Chapter 6 113
Digitally Shifting to Create Communities of Learning
- Systemic constraints limit what we can achieve in instruction
- Digital tools have the power to bend those constraints

PART III
Mapping New Realities for the Digital Age

Chapter 7 129
Creating Learner-Centered Virtual Environments
- Tools should be adapted to meet the needs of instruction, not the other way around
- Teachers should advocate for tools that match their pedagogical strategies

Chapter 8 145
Mapping the Digital Learning Journey
- Digital tools provide us with an infinite learning canvas
- Teachers are natural navigators, mapmakers, and storytellers

Chapter 9 161
Designing Communities in a Digital World
- Hybrid Plus provides a framework for thinking about learning tasks critically
- It is based on the need to create Communities of Practice

Final Thoughts 179
Teaching is Evergreen

Bibliography 185

Acknowledgments 189

About the Author 191

> *"No operation extends with any certainty beyond the first encounter with the main body of the enemy."*
> *– Helmuth von Moltke*

Foreword

Exiting the Pandemic:
A Model for Education Going Forward

There is no question in my mind that my class is better today than it was before the pandemic took us out of the physical world. I began this process several years ago, when I tore down my instruction to its bare bones. I then examined everything I had been doing for almost two decades. I asked myself questions like "How does doing X contribute to the goals I've set for my students?" If I could not answer that question, I discarded the action or adapted it to a different media where it was going to be more effective. It took a year's worth of work and some semi-patient students, but at the end of my deconstruction process I had a pretty good idea of how to fine tune my pedagogical activities to meet the students where they were. I also had a fairly precise idea of what each "tool" I was using was doing and whether I needed technology or human interaction to make it do what I wanted it to.

My pedagogy shifted decisively when I started this process of self-examination. A deliberate focus on student-centered learning pushed me from a 1.0 version of my class to a 2.0 version of it. The class became a semester-long project that the students chose for themselves, instead of random chunks of information that *I* thought would be meaningful to them. When the pandemic hit, it forced me to take a lot of the pieces I had been meaning to digitize and finally put them online, leaving concentrated human interactions to scaffold everything else. The structure of the 2.0 class was largely unaffected, but the pandemic forced me to apply new and better digital tools. This final step made the class stronger than ever. I will not be going back.

My experience stands in stark contrast to that of many of my colleagues. I have seen far too many approaches in dealing with the pandemic that relied upon optimistic expectations instead of antifragile planning to steer educational institutions through the crisis. The one thing that characterizes most of these approaches is that they relied on institutional and technological responses to the challenges of remote learning instead of starting with the kinds of root-level pedagogical explorations that motivated my own class redesign. The result has been, as of this writing in early November 2020, a hodgepodge of approaches that can charitably described as reactive and has led to a degradation of quality in many instances.

Any reasonable observer in March would have recognized that the messiest outcome, a scenario where schools try to open up only to unexpectedly shut down when COVID-19 cases spiked – what Bryan Alexander describes as "Toggle Term,"[1] – was actually the most optimistic and also the most likely version of what the Fall Semester would look like. And yet, almost no one

---

[1] https://bryanalexander.org/future-of-education/higher-education-in-fall-2020-three-pandemic-scenarios/

realistically prepared for that eventuality. The extreme uncertainties of Toggle Term require a profoundly human approach to sustain communities of learning. Instead, we saw many institutions, ranging from school districts to elite universities, implement complex technologies, fail to adapt fundamental instructional practices, and generally increase the isolation of learners, when precisely the opposite was called for.

Why was that? One answer, derived from systems thinking, is that that scenario seemed to require responses that challenged too many paradigms of industrial education. These included funding formulas based on physical attendance, mass high-stakes testing, large lecture halls, residential dormitories, sports, and international visa requirements. Many of those were going to be challenged regardless and were already overdue for some serious rethinking. None of them are central to the mission of learning. All should take a back seat to the needs of students trying to get on with their learning journeys, often in the face of incredible obstacles.

The other critical mistake that has come out of this crisis was the belief that "technology will save us all." There is no question but that technology has provided us tremendous affordances and opportunities that allowed us to Band-Aid the system in the spring. However, technology-first systems are incredibly brittle, both from a technical perspective (prone to breakdowns under stress), but also from the perspective of systems of learning. Design teaches us that the most effective solutions are built up through a critical examination of the needs, goals, and capabilities of the user, in this case the teacher and the learner. Understanding what we know about teaching should be a departure point for every technological and organizational (systemic) decision we make. After safety considerations stemming from the pandemic, which are likely to be short- to medium-range in nature, the long-term disruption to both present and future learners must be of paramount concern.

This book is in part a compilation of my reflections on teaching and learning during the pandemic. It is based on my experience of 40 years as a technologist and practical experience teaching government courses at a community college. Many of the conclusions are also a product of the work being done for my forthcoming volume, *Discovering Digital Humanity*, which outlines a set of principles to inform our relationship with systems of technology. What makes this book different is that it starts and ends with teaching. Its strategies begin with pedagogical concerns and then explore how those pedagogical concerns interact with technology as well as the larger systems of mass education that we have constructed. While some of the explorations touch on altering larger systems so that they are more in tune with 21st Century economic and social realities, this book is designed for the teacher to help him or her to navigate their learners through a universe of shifting sands.

While it uses the 2020 pandemic as a launching point for its deeper explorations, the book is not just meant as a roadmap through the pandemic. It is intended as a launching point for a series of overdue discussions about how we can optimize teaching and learning by taking full advantage of the opportunities that the Digital Age offers us. It is time to realize that we are no longer hostage to the dehumanizing realities of industrial education with its implicit assumptions that students are nothing more than widgets moving down a highly imperfect assembly line.

The danger now lies in losing sight of the individual as the pandemic has eaten away at the human glue around the edges, which worked to counter the dehumanizing effects of 500-person lecture halls, standardized testing, and distanced education based on those assumptions. Deep learning responds to the needs of the learner. Institutions should do the same, but the teacher forms the critical nexus through all of this. It is to them that I dedicate this work.

Introduction

A Crisis Design Primer for Teachers

You have just been through 8 hours of unremitting stress flying your bomber over Germany, being shot at, and just keeping your plane in the air. As you approach your airfield in Southern England, you pull the lever to lower your landing gear and listen for the satisfying chirp of rubber on the runway that indicates you are home. Instead, your senses are greeted with a rending crash as your bomber careens over the asphalt runway. Your belly gunner is probably dead, and your plane is a wreck. The problem? The knob that lowers your flaps is right next to that which raises your landing gear. Instead of slowing your speed and increasing the lift of your wings the nearly identical knob has raised your landing gear.[2]

Teaching feels a lot like that sometimes. As someone who spends a lot of time designing for a lot of possible outcomes in my teaching, every semester I have had my share of unexpected belly landings. Over the years, however, I have worked hard to bring to bear a range of experiences and research from a broad spectrum of disciplines to constantly refine the design of my class. Part

---

[2] Kuang, Cliff, "How the Dumb Design of a WW II Plane Led to the Macintosh, *Wired*, 11/13/19 https://bit.ly/2UdHpT5

of this is technological, as I have sought to examine the tools that I can bring to bear on a wide range of circumstances. Part of this is structural, as I have sought to understand how schools and classrooms operate as systems of human interaction. And part of this is instructional, as I have constantly sought to learn and adapt human-centric pedagogical strategies. As a result, when the pandemic swept across the educational landscape, my classes were more prepared than most to weather its disruptions.

In a 2012 book, Nicholas Taleb, the systems theorist responsible for the term "black swan," added a new term to our vocabulary. He wrote, "Some things benefit from shocks; they thrive and grow when exposed to volatility, randomness, disorder, and stressors and love adventure, risk, and uncertainty. Yet, in spite of the ubiquity of the phenomenon, there is no word for the exact opposite of fragile. Let us call it antifragile."[3] The pandemic made my instruction even more antifragile as I gamed out and applied the principles outlined in this book to work whether we are meeting fully online, partially online in small groups, or in more traditional hybrid modalities. This book builds on the principles and approaches outlined in my forthcoming volume *Discovering Digital Humanity*, but that book is a book of ideas. This book is intended first and foremost as a set of practical steps that can be taken to make any class antifragile during the pandemic and beyond. As COVID-19 shut down in-person instruction across education, we must take the time to grasp at the right levers and to design systems so that our students aren't forced to suffer the consequences of our

---

[3] Taleb, Nassim Nicholas. *Antifragile: Things That Gain from Disorder* (Incerto). Random House Publishing Group. Kindle Edition

mistakes. Learning is antifragile. Many of the systems designed around it are not.

This book may have been written in the context of the COVID-19 pandemic and its effect on education. However, its underlying principles are the result of decades of work and, more importantly, were always directed toward a larger set of hurdles that have only been exposed by the impact that the crisis has had on our approaches to teaching and learning: the impact that the Digital Age is having, and will have, on our Industrial Age educational models. Some see this as a threatening development, attacking familiar patterns of how we go about our day-to-day tasks as teachers. I have always seen this as a tremendous opportunity to augment our ability to teach future generations of teachers and learners. In much the same way as the chalkboard ushered in an era of mass teaching, the vast array of digital tools, some of which are decades old, will usher in a new era of learner-centric, humanistic teaching and learning. We all got into education to reach others. Properly applied and designed sets of digital tools make that easier, not harder. Most of the negative experiences from the emergency pandemic measures virtually all institutions have been forced to adopt have come from badly thought through tool design and selection as well as a fear of grasping unexpected opportunities that might arise from the altered landscape.

At its heart this book is about insights I have gained from designing systems (classes, programs, buildings, technology) and which I have applied to my own classes. I eat my own dog food and have learned a lot of hard lessons over the years from failed experiments, which makes the point that you learn a lot more from failure than from success. My frustrations over the years, coupled with optimism stemming from my long association with technology has led me to constantly seek to refine what I was doing in class and how I was doing it. I constantly consider not only how technology could make my life easier as a teacher but what opportunities there were for my students to learn differently and more effectively than the mass production techniques that have characterized so much of education for much of the last century and to this day.

All learning requires a framework to give it a useful context. Otherwise, it's just a game of Jeopardy trivia. Like what I ask of my students, I have borrowed and adapted a set of useful frameworks to help me through this journey of exploration and experimentation. In my government classes I ask my students to engage in a process of design as a semester-long project. I engage in this process myself as I seek to make the best use of the tools and techniques developed around the world to further my teaching. And this book is also fundamentally one of design. Each chapter begins with a strategy and several concrete action items that flow from it. These "actions items" are intended to be something an individual teacher can implement. The remainder of each chapter explores some aspect of the challenge more deeply.

The Nine Strategies:

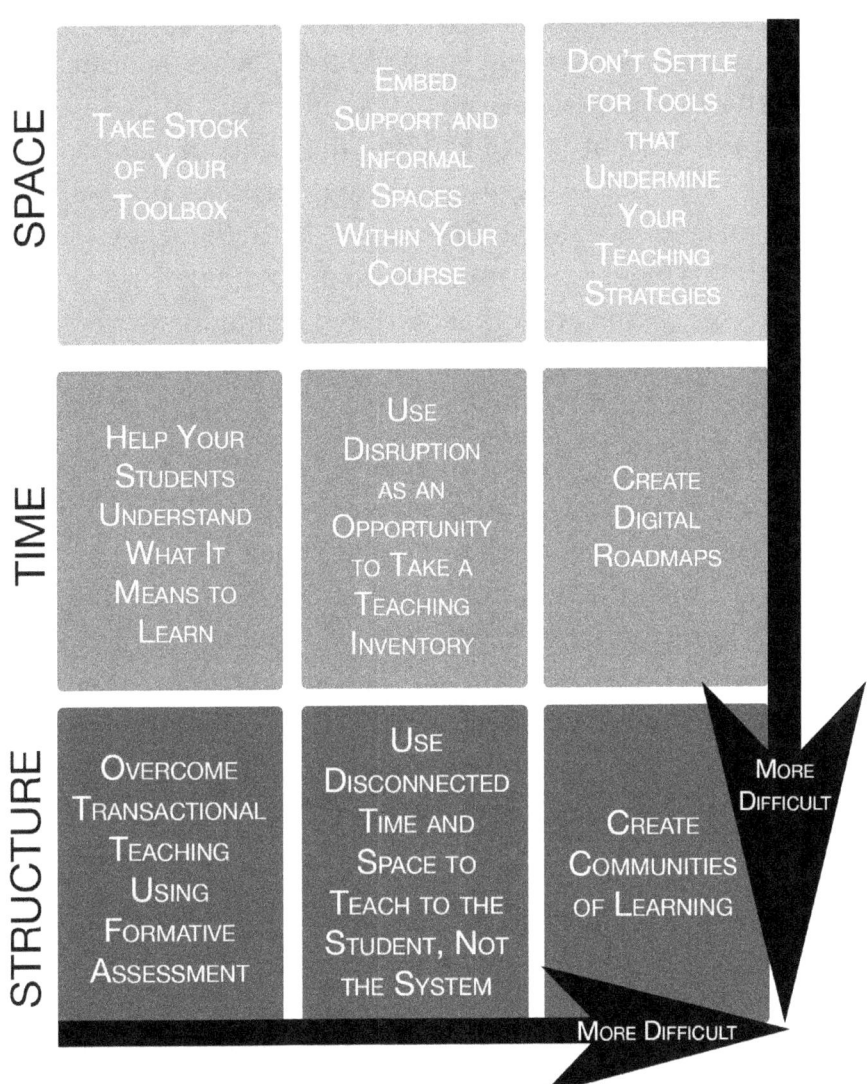

We often overlook how broadly design impacts our lives. As Don Norman points out, "All artificial things are designed."[4] It impacts every level of the teaching and learning experience. Design touches the layout of our classrooms, the digital tools we use, and the very nature of semesters, class sessions, and curriculum. All of these are being tested right now, including the limits of classroom design. In order to begin any design process, no matter how rushed, we must first understand the goals and constraints of what we are trying to do. Imagine a scenario where the government has declared gatherings over 10 people inadvisable due to the pandemic. It is mid-semester. Go.

When we asked thousands of instructors and millions of students to go online with little or no preparation, we saw lots and lots of crash landings as all grasped for unfamiliar tools and struggled to survive in poorly designed systems ill-equipped to adapt to rapidly shifting circumstances on the ground. There are many levels of intertwingled (intertwined and intermingled) systems (as Ted Nelson would put it) where poor design can fail us.

As teachers, we control, to a greater or lesser extent, the design of our daily lessons, course structure, and the tools we bring to bear on the problems of teaching and learning. This book is a design book for you to begin or continue your own explorations as teaching embodies what Ann Pendleton-Jullian and John Seely Brown call "emergent design."[5] In other words, it forms a set of

---

[4] Norman, *The Design of Everyday Things*, Basic Books, 2013, p. 4.
https://books.google.com/books/about/The_Design_of_Everyday_Things.html?id=b09jQgAACAAJ
[5] *Design Unbound*, MIT Press, 2018

wicked problems that demand open-ended design processes. My work as a teacher is subject to constant modification and improvement as I create bubbles of learning that I hope will catch all or most of my students. Students bring with them their own systems of learning that are constrained or facilitated by their individual circumstances, ranging from the amount of time and support they have for independent work in their personal lives, their opportunities to interact with their peers constructively, and the structure of the rest of their academic experiences. This is a never-ending process. One of my favorite quotes from fantasy author Patrick Rothfuss encapsulates my perspective on this as both a teacher and a learner: "It's the questions we can't answer that teach us the most. They teach us how to think. If you give a man an answer, all he gains is a little fact. But give him a question and he'll look for his own answers."[6] This book is very much intended to provoke you into searching for your own answers.

    At the highest level, we run up against the systemic construct that we call the semester/credit-hour/contact hour class. These are designed realities, as is the whole system of grades, transcripts, GPAs, etc. Norman would describe these as "services, lectures, rules and procedures, and the organizational rules of businesses and governments do not have physical mechanisms, but their rules of operation have to be designed, sometimes informally, sometimes precisely recorded and specified."[7]

---

[6] *The Wise Man's Fear,* 2011
[7] Norman, *ibid*

There are limits. As teachers we must consider the fundamental design questions that underlie many of these kinds of realities. To what extent do we have the power to alter them? What are the boundaries of our design playground? There is pressure to keep the larger system intact and, as a result, there are many systemic factors that prevent us from simply blowing the "traditional" academic structure up. Instead of addressing the systemic paradigm, the initial reaction was to lean on technology to simply move all "instruction online" or "have in-person classes" with very little discussion of the nuances implied by both approaches. At most institutions the systemic design paradigm wasn't challenged and these kinds of questions were simply not being asked. Many of the decisions taken during Covid Spring shifted the burden of design from the administrators to the faculty who had to deal with a new set of constraints in the design of how they interact with their students.

The consequences of those decisions are still being evaluated, but early returns are not encouraging. By shifting systemic burdens downward onto faculty, parents, and students, we virtually guaranteed that the most vulnerable students (and faculty) would break first. Putting the burden of adjustment on the instructor was in itself a design decision. It reshaped the parameters and constraints of those struggling with classroom organization in a radically reshaped world. On a classroom level, faculty had to consider the systems of learning they were setting up for their students and how these might be disrupted by a shift of modality and related tools for learning. What used to occur as a casual conversation within the class or outside the class now had to be intermediated by technology. Bad technology design inevitably introduced barriers to communication. It is, however, important to remember that physical meetings also impose barriers in that they involve putting people together in the same place at the same time, but these are design challenges we implicitly manage.

As we explore in detail in Chapter 2, all instruction is a form of designed conversation. First, as mentioned, there are direct conversations between the teacher and the student, among the students (peers), and between the student and the teacher. Then there are indirect conversations, usually taking the form of assessments. These can also be interactions between students and teachers as well as peers. They require rapid feedback to the learner. Finally, there is the preservation of active learning, which involves immediate, internal feedback to the student. In other words, a conversation that the learner has with his or herself.

Moving instruction online carries with it at least two dangers to these paths of communication, particularly in a time of social isolation. First of all, the isolation itself must be considered and acknowledged. Online learning, as it is usually designed, is often a solitary process. Impersonal bulletin boards often offer little or no incentive to participate unless compelled to do so by extrinsic motivators. As I once said to an instructor in the early days of Facebook as he was considering using it for his class, "no one wants to go to a cocktail party with their parents." Don't expect our students to rush to primitive communication devices like discussion boards. Discussion boards *can* be a vibrant form of peer interaction, but the students have to have their own intrinsic reasons for going there. That's extremely hard to achieve with the vast majority of K-20 students.

Related to this problem, and the second big issue, is the lack of informal learning in most Learning Management Systems. When I say, "informal" learning, I mean spaces that allow students to informally congregate with one another without the intervention of teachers. Peer conversations such as study groups can form in these spaces. More importantly, they may give isolated students (aka, people) the ability to socialize in a society practicing social distancing. Consider how this might be accomplished online. Does your videoconferencing tool give students the ability to form their own groups? Could this reach beyond the traditional course shell to encompass other sections or even other disciplines? Done correctly, this could encourage students to spend more of their online time with each other rather than with random strangers on Snapchat.

In addition to space-time issues, technology itself can introduce unfamiliar barriers to student access for both the student and the teacher/designer. In a 2018 article, researchers at the University of Indiana concluded that technological barriers are not evenly distributed throughout our student bodies. In a study of Indiana students researchers discovered that "roughly 20% of respondents had difficulty maintaining access to technology (e.g., broken hardware, data limits, connectivity problems, etc.). Students of lower socio-economic status and students of color disproportionately experienced hardships, and reliance on poorly functioning laptops was associated with lower grade point averages."[8]

---

[8] Gonzales, A. L., McCrory Calarco, J., & Lynch, T. (2020). Technology Problems and Student Achievement Gaps: A Validation and Extension of the Technology Maintenance Construct. Communication Research, 47(5), 750–770. https://doi.org/10.1177/0093650218796366

And so we have another set of unexpected variables to our design challenge.

We are bending instruction. When things are bent, basic functions of their design come to the fore. Is what is being bent flexible or is it brittle? Can it be adapted into another form and how does that change its form or efficacy of purpose? By looking at it differently, can we see new opportunities for its use? While learning is a process, how we get there is fundamentally a function of design. This logic applies to the modalities we apply to the communication, assessment, and scope of learning in our classes. The good news is that we have a vast new range of digital tools that create design possibilities in and for our classes and this gives us many new tools to use as we navigate the difficult process of learning with our students. Understanding their basic functionalities and how they fit into the overall system of what we are trying to do is going to be key to adapting teaching and learning to our profoundly reshaped social world. It's time to roll up our sleeves and get to work. It is my hope that this book will help show you where to begin.

PART I

Overcoming Transactional Teaching

Using Tools and Transparency

- *Use Tools to Teach*
- *Teach Learning*
- *Create Deep Understanding*

Chapter 1
Use Tasks to Drive Your Toolsets

Teaching fundamentally boils down to communication. We communicate ideas, we communicate skills, and we communicate achievement. In the 1960s Marshall McLuhan wrote extensively about how media shapes the messages it conveys. His famous dictum, "the medium is the message" captured a fundamental reality that *how* we communicate is often as important as *what* we intend to communicate. As our access to media has expanded in the Digital Age, we often forget this and simply assume that what we do in a physical environment will automatically translate to what we perceive as an analogous medium. As a consequence, we repeatedly make what I like to call "McLuhanesque mistakes" and transfer things back-and-forth from various media without having a clear appreciation of the interaction between that media and the intent of our communication. Sometimes a car is better than a boat. Sometimes a boat is better than a car. It all comes down to context. Sometimes persistent, asynchronous interaction is better than live feedback. Sometimes live feedback is better than disconnected, asynchronous interaction. It all comes down to context. If teaching and learning is to manage in a pandemic and beyond, then we need to become masters of all of the different means of transporting students on their learning journeys. If anything has become clear over the last few months, it's that we won't always be able to predict the context under which they are traveling.

When analyzing tools and media it's essential to start with the task you are trying to accomplish and work your way upwards. Break down your activities to their smallest component and ask yourself the following questions:

1) What is the pedagogical task I am trying to achieve? Be as specific as possible. Example: *I want my students to collect information from public sources about a political issue they are interested in and analyze it critically.*

2) How did I do this in an in-person class synchronously? Example: *We analyzed sources found in class as a group and tried to connect them with concepts that we were learning about government.*

3) How could this be done asynchronously? Example: *Collection was already an asynchronous activity. Sources could be analyzed asynchronously in a discussion topic. However, the immediacy of the discussion will be lost.*
4) What kinds of synchronous tools do I use for this in the classroom? Example: *I use a large screen to display the sources to the class to facilitate discussion and highlight certain parts of the argument.*
5) What kinds of asynchronous or distant tools can I use to replicate the experience? Example: *Videoconference restores some element of the live conversation but students have an easier time hiding during the experience. Complementing this with a reflective essay might be one way to get students to engage asynchronously with a synchronous event, especially one they can review asynchronously (persistence can help here).*
6) What kinds of opportunities does digital create?
7) Examples: *Persistence of even "live" events (assuming they're recorded) allows post hoc review and meta-analysis of the activity.*

Create a chart to work across tasks and build tools around needs.

Task ⇒	Synchronous Activity ⇒	Asynchronous Analog ⇒	Synchronous Tools ⇒	Remote/Asynchronous Tools Analog ⇒	Digital Opportunities
EXAMPLE Critically evaluate political information from sources of public information ⇒	EXAMPLE Upload sources to shared repository, in-class group review with active instructor participation ⇒	EXAMPLE Discuss sources on discussion board ⇒	EXAMPLE Display - web connection. ⇒	EXAMPLE Reflective essay on how analysis was done. Recorded live discussion - Persistent reflective activity - Screen sharing ⇒	EXAMPLE - Review and reflection - Persistence - Sharing of sources - Persistence allows easier formative reflection - Concept mapping sources to reference material

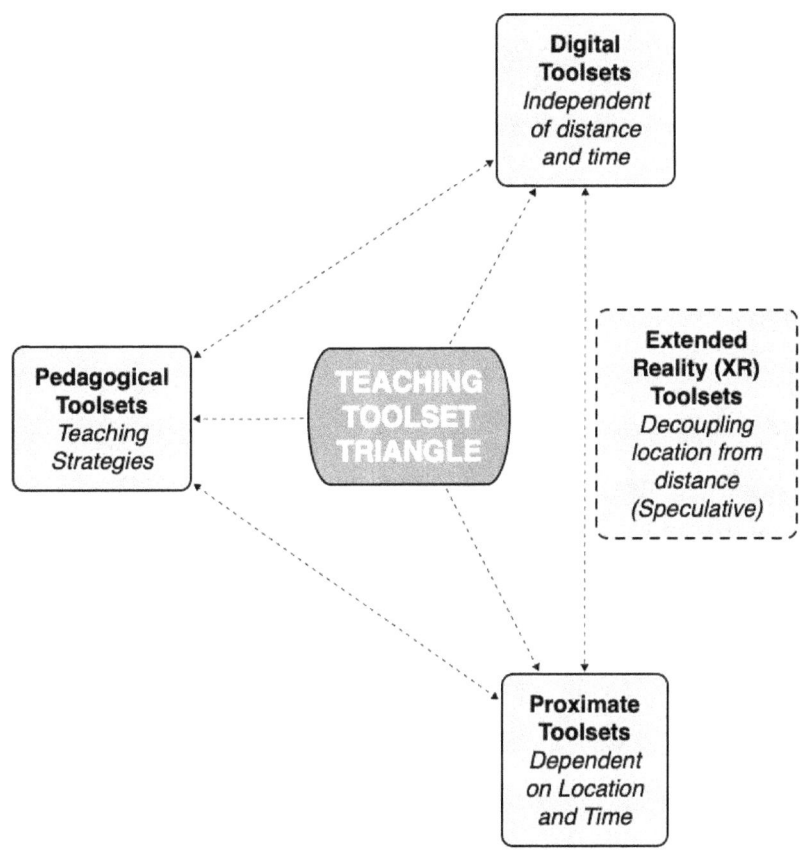

The Teaching Toolset Triangle (T3)

The Teaching Toolset Triangle
Building Up Instead of Building Down

I have always been a technological interloper. I have used computers for all of my serious work since the early 80s and so when I started teaching 20 years later, I could not understand why people refused to grasp the tools at hand. My very first semester I was lugging a large projector along with my laptop out to temporary classrooms at a high school for teaching dual credit because the tools in the room were inadequate for the kinds of stories I wanted to tell. I felt like a pack mule, but it was in service of what I wanted to share with my students. In those days it was the ability to share graphics without a bunch of handouts and maybe some primitive internet sites.

The other thing that computers allowed me to do was use multimedia strategically using short clips from movies, documentaries, and news stories that I deployed organically within my lessons. I even went so far as to create a DVD of clips for my colleagues to do the same. Technology allowed me to share what I was doing in my classes in ways that were impossible without digital tools. The point is that I wasn't using technology to show off. I was using it to bang at the walls of my classroom and to show my students that government was a living, breathing thing, not some dry chapter in a textbook.

The spread of COVID-19 had a dramatic effect on our delivery of instruction and is likely to **continue** to do so for the foreseeable future. *If you lose access to a large swath of in-person tools, you need to carefully analyze how all of your tools work in order to maximize the* *impact of those tools you have left in the toolbox.* We need a meta-tool to analyze the toolbox itself.

One problem is that we take most of our tools for granted. They are part of systems of action that we have maintained and adapted over the years from older tools. We rarely reflect on the way these very tools shape our actions. COVID-19 has smashed many of these assumptions but even without the virus, a reckoning with our expanded toolsets in both learning and innovation was way overdue.

Even with the best of intentions, teaching often struggles with inadequate or badly matched tools. It is only when we have some **understanding** of our pedagogical departure points (real or desired) that we can start to evaluate the impact that our various learning environments and their constituent toolsets have on the success or failure to execute our teaching strategies within them. Until very recently these toolsets were extremely limited by the technology available to us. Classrooms consisted of blackboards, maybe some sort of projection device (e.g. overhead projector), desks and chairs. There wasn't much opportunity to customize the environment that students operated in under these circumstances.

Over the last 20 years, however, we have seen an explosion of new tools, both physical and digital. However, their selection and implementation have often been subject to haphazard processes. We have built our educational environments as if we were building a car one piece at a time. When physical campuses suddenly shut down in March 2020, we essentially put the pedal to the metal on this jalopy, crossed our fingers, and hoped for the best.

One of the lessons that became obvious throughout this experience is that **learning** is not perceived as a collection of parts. Environments are not perceived as collections of various technologies. The experience is viewed holistically by the learner. Implicit and subliminal cues provide a general impression of the purpose of any space, whether that is physical or digital in nature. These spaces all send messages about what is important and what is not. As an artist, I have a deep understanding that the intention behind a message is rarely the message communicated, assuming that there was any coherent intention in the first place.

Even spaces and technology that are explicitly focused and coherent can unintentionally bias what goes on there in particular pedagogical directions. **Conway's Law** states that, "Any organization that designs a system (defined broadly) will produce a design whose structure is a copy of the organization's communication structure."[9] In other words, organizational processes rather than intentional design often shape the design of the toolsets available to teachers and that in turn shapes the product, learning, that emerges. The results are predictable. Systems of space and technology shape the boundaries and expectations of what is possible within a given space or using a particular tool. Most teachers and students will tend to adapt themselves accordingly instead of insisting that the environment conform to their needs.

There are a vast number of interactions that occur in the learning process, whether that be in the classroom, online, or in life in general. In order to start solving this puzzle in any sort of rigorous fashion, we first have to

---

[9] http://www.melconway.com/Home/Conways_Law.html

deconstruct our pedagogical strategies in order to understand how the kinds of conversations that are going on between teachers and students shape the intended shape of learning. We go into this in greater detail in Chapter 2.

Second, as we plan to confront the crisis and maintain our economic and educational futures *it has never been more critical to understand the expanding universe of tools now available to us to communicate and share ideas with one another*. This is a process that the Teaching Toolset Triangle systemizes. It is designed to provide a rubric for evaluating and selecting tools (and collections of tools) that have the capacity to reshape instruction and organizational innovation.

In the short term, these strategies can be directed toward making instruction more **antifragile** in the face of institutional and societal uncertainties such as the pandemic spread of a virus that unexpectedly shuts down large portions of our physical infrastructure. It would be compounding tragedy if we did not learn from this time of adversity and use what we have learned to examine those parts of the system that don't make sense anymore. Those organizations that do so will thrive. Those that don't are likely to be crippled by the experience of the new realities of a post-pandemic world.

Developing a Rubric for Assessing the Tools We Use to Teach and Learn

We view our educational environments holistically. When a teacher and student enter a space, whether that space is a physical room or a virtual tool, it tends to define their perceptions of possible interactions within that space. Rarely do we critically examine how different kinds of tools shape our collective experiences or conversations.

Consider what kinds of questions might be raised by the three "spaces" pictured:

- What kind of instruction is most likely to occur in this space?
- What kind of instruction is the student likely to expect when entering this space?
- What kind of instruction is the faculty member likely to gravitate toward when confronted with this teaching environment?

Consider for a moment the explicit and implicit messages that these spaces are sending to those interacting within them.

This same kind of analysis can be applied to our interactions with virtual spaces and how they interact with our physical environments.

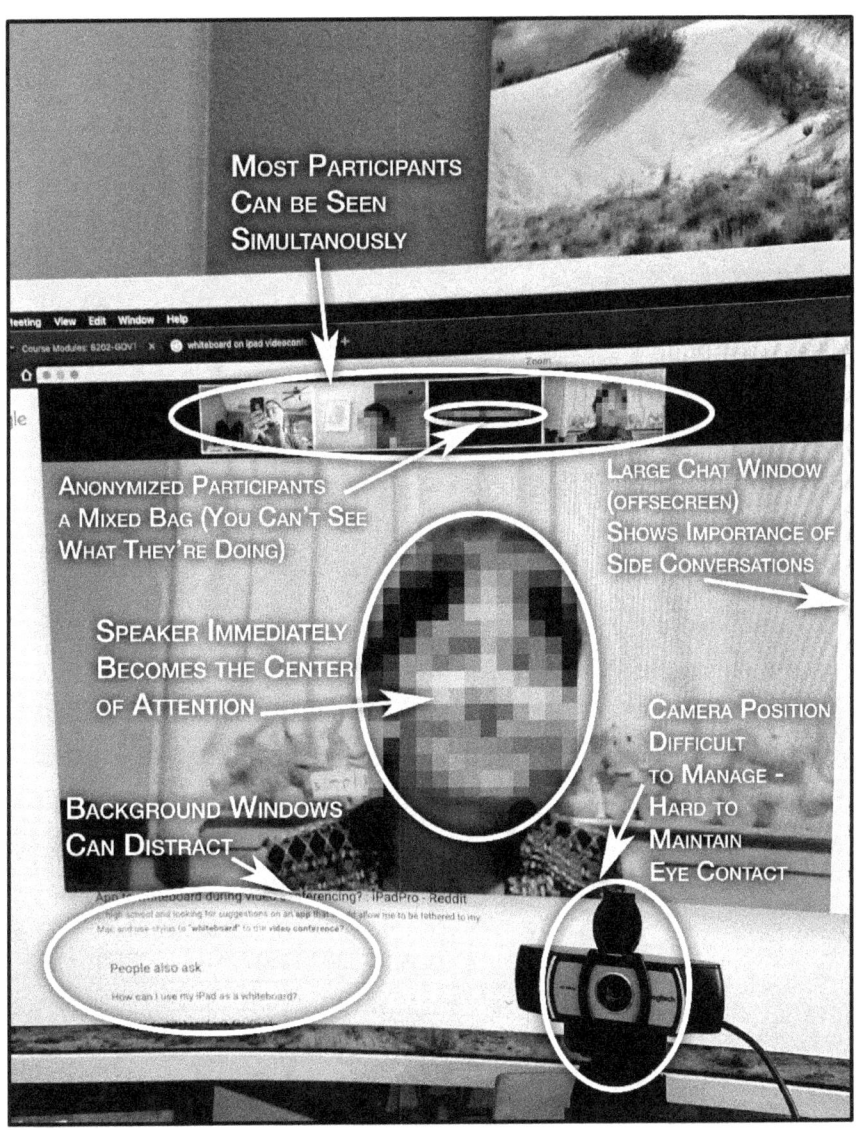

Even as available tools have proliferated since the blackboard-projector-desk paradigm, our selection and purchasing of systems have by and large been dominated by the non-instructional parts of the institution. The somewhat predictable result has been a hodgepodge of experimental spaces designed with little regard to the actual teaching modalities that were being attempted there. Couple this with the problem that most teachers, much less students, know little about design, and you have a recipe for ineffective sets of tools. Mismatches between modalities and environments inevitably resulted in calls for changing human software through "professional development" in order to adapt the faculty (and students) to new technologies. This is fundamentally backwards. Humans should dictate their technological needs based on their needs and goals; not the other way around. We need a tool to help us figure out our tools. The intent of the Teaching Toolset Triangle (T3) is to design that tool.

To simplify the process, it is best to break down tools into sets that have similar characteristics. However, note that there is considerable overlap between the three categories and no tool, much less category, clearly sets us on pathways toward a particular pedagogical mode. The intent here is to develop a sophisticated perception of shades of gray, not try to get to black-and-white solutions.

Proximate/Physical Toolsets:
What shapes our synchronous environments?

Characteristics

- **Conversations** – Physical environments allow impromptu and planned conversations to take place with immediate feedback and interaction. At present, they are the best platform for engaging in this kind of activity.
- **Immediacy** – Physical environments allow for students to be fully "in-the-moment" at a level more difficult to achieve in virtual environments
- **Human Contact** – As Lave and Wenger point out, "learning is an integral and inseparable aspect of social practice."[10] Physical spaces allow the teacher, mentors, and peers to interact on an authentic level that transcends what is possible in virtual environments.
- **Performance** – As Shakespeare wrote, "All the world's a stage, and all the men and women merely players." There is an element of theater in all physical interactions that is accentuated when those interactions happen live in the physical world.

---

[10] Lave and Wenger, 1991, p. 31.
https://www.cambridge.org/us/academic/subjects/psychology/developmental-psychology/situated-learning-legitimate-peripheral-participation

Examples of Physical/Proximate Toolsets

- Formal Learning Spaces
    - Projection/Display
        - Large (Faculty)
        - Small (Student)
    - Whiteboard
        - Large (Faculty)
        - Small (Student)
    - Mobile furniture
    - Variable-sized meeting spaces
    - Student Use Science Equipment
    - Student Use Computing Equipment

- Informal Learning Spaces
    - Student-Accessible Display
    - Whiteboards
    - Mobile Furniture
    - Group Demarcation
    - Quiet Study
    - Ubiquitous Computing
    - Faculty consultation/meetings
    - Support Services Areas
        - Personal (Counseling)
        - Information (Library)
        - Design (MakerSpace)
        - Instructional (Tutoring)

Virtual Toolsets:
How does digital change the environment?

Characteristics

- **Persistence** – Unless they are recorded (and then often put onto "virtual" platforms) human activities in physical environments are ephemeral. Content and interactions situated online are accessible long after the fact. This is a significant advantage to the persistence of digital footprints. Properly configured, this presents the student with the opportunity of reflecting on his or her learning journey.
- **Automation of Processes** – Computation can aid and automate processes such as record-keeping and calculation, freeing up instructor time for more creative activities related to teaching and learning.
- **Asynchronicity** – The persistence of online content and some activities allow for considerable asynchronicity of student activity. This can constitute a significant benefit to those students juggling other responsibilities such as work, family, or athletics. However, there is a cost in the form of isolating the learner who is working at a different time as his or her peers and this can have significant negative impact on the efficacy of peer-intensive teaching modalities.

A Special Note on Virtual Toolsets: As is the case with physical spaces, the subliminal messages that virtual spaces send out significantly impact the type of learning that is likely to occur there. Also, like physical spaces, subtle differences in user experience have significantly impacted the experience of both teacher and learner. However, unlike physical spaces, virtual spaces are easily redesigned and often subtle design choices can loom large in the more disconnected world of virtual toolsets. Therefore, the model makes some generalizations in the name of simplicity. Individual platforms, such as Learning Management Systems and Videoconferencing Systems deserve detailed exploration of the biases of a given product toward one form of teaching and learning versus the others. Also, subtle changes in the software can result in significant changes in the user experience, altering the analysis of the systems in question. Pedagogical questions must be central to the design, selection, and adoption of these tools just as they are with the selection of tables and chairs. Mindful design is even more essential in a fluid, data-driven environment.

Examples of Digital/Virtual Toolsets
- LMS Tools
    - Assessments
    - Quizzes
    - Tests
    - Submissions
    - Discussions
    - Conference
    - Content
- Web Tools
    - Blogs
    - Concept Mapping
    - Drawing
    - Image Editing
    - Coding
- Google
    - Drive
    - Docs
    - Sheets
    - Slides
- Video
    - Kaltura
    - YouTube
    - Adobe Spark

- Videoconferencing
    - Zoom
    - Microsoft Teams
    - Google Meets
    - WebEx
    - Shindig
- Online Textbook Sites
- Open Educational Resources

XR/AR/VR Toolsets: Best of Both Environments?

XR systems are still in their infancy, especially when it comes to user/instructor developed content. However, like other, similar technologies in the past, these barriers will start to come down and it is possible to envision XR systems that are as easy to customize as Minecraft or a WordPress site. XR systems are starting to offer distinct, high touch, high feel experiences that have the potential to bridge some of the gaps between physical and virtual environments. What follows are some speculative ideas of what is being developed and/or might be possible within the next 5 years using XR technology. It is possible to construct the same mapping of pedagogical strategies onto these toolsets but until practical experience becomes more common these will be difficult to evaluate in the manner of the tools listed earlier in the model.

Characteristics

- **Adaptability** – XR has the potential to be as adaptable as any other well-designed digital platform, allowing for the instantaneous modification of environments, to cite just one example.
- **Persistence** – Like other digital tools, XR environments can be persistent and easily duplicated once created.
- **Immersion** – Like physical spaces, XR environments offer the capability to fully immerse an individual in an activity or environment.
- **Physical/Digital Fusion (AR)** – The Augmented Reality subset of XR allows users to overlay a digital footprint over their perceptions of the physical environment like a customizable heads up display on a car.
- **Blend Synchronicity with Asynchronicity** – XR environments may blend the immediacy of synchronous interactions with others in the environment with the ability to record or freeze interactions within that environment for asynchronous future analysis and learning.

Examples of XR Toolsets

Augmented Reality
- Science Fieldwork
- Workforce/Training
- Augmented Presentation

Immersive Environments (Virtual Reality)
- Experiential Immersion
- Videoconferencing Plus
- Immersive Shadowing

Immersive Problem-Solving (Virtual Reality)
- VR Making
- 3D Concept Mapping
- Immersive Labs

Applying Insights from the Teaching Toolset Triangle

While this chapter seems to explicitly focus on a list of tools, it is important not to take our eyes off the ball. We need to recognize that this strategy depends fundamentally on mindfulness in what we are doing as we attempt to adapt our instruction under difficult circumstances. The Triangle is a tool for deconstructing tools so that they can be applied in the most efficient ways possible to a wide range of circumstances. The insights of this chapter are based on the fundamental departure point that our teaching tasks should drive our teaching environments, no matter where those environments are constructed. The only way that we will achieve mastery over our tools, however, is by taking a hard look at the tasks that we perform as teachers. It is to that subject that we now turn.

Chapter 2

Listening and Learning in an Era of Social Distancing

If teaching is a process of communication, that communication takes place in a set of conversations that every student experiences. As Laurillard's Conversational Framework describes the process, these conversations take place between the teacher and the student, between the student and his or her peers, and within the mind of the student.[11] One of the mistakes that our systems of education make is that they focus too much on the process of education and too little on the practice of learning. Teachers and students alike often miss the "why" of the

---

[11] Laurillard, Diana, 2003, 2007, 2009
https://books.google.com/books/about/Rethinking_University_Teaching.html?id=99eQakJyAj4C
https://discovery.ucl.ac.uk/id/eprint/10000627/1/Mobile_C6_Laurillard.pdf
https://hal.archives-ouvertes.fr/hal-00592750/document

tasks that are undertaken on a day-to-day basis in every classroom. The most important conversation that a student has is the one going on inside his or her head. If the process of getting through school is a mystery to them then it also becomes a game without real meaning. Their lack of understanding of the importance of learning versus "getting an education" leads to a range of pernicious effects including indifference, gaming grades, and cheating. We must prioritize changing these internal conversations if we are to create learners out of our students.

Times of crisis prompt us to take a hard look at what we are doing, what works, and what doesn't. Treating students in bewildering times like they're rats in a maze is a sure way for them to become lost. The COVID-19 Crisis, coupled with the Digital Transition, has exposed all of the cracks in our learning systems, the implicit assumptions, the wasted time and energy, and flawed pedagogical strategies. When the car is stripped to its bare bones, it's easy to see what parts are working and what parts aren't. This is an opportunity to make this process transparent to the learners and make them a part of reconstructing systems of learning in a post-pandemic world.

This should be viewed as yet another digital opportunity. Embrace the new digital reality. Reveal the wizard behind the curtain and make it clear that in the end they have the power to make the journey, not us. We're just there to help. Explain why we have in-class meetings. Let them explain why they do or don't work for them. Work through alternatives together. Bring your expertise to bear to keep the course on track, not to dictate outcomes.

One way to do this is to spend most of your synchronous time reviewing both individual and group progress in very concrete terms. One of the "revelations" of the online transitions that occurred in Spring 2020 was that giving live lectures is not a very effective interactive strategy online. This yet another example of how the digital world has laid bare something that was already widely known. We compensated for this in live classrooms by "working the room." However, in an online environment most students quickly became passive participants. It is extremely hard to "read the room" when the room consists of a set of black boxes in a videoconferencing space. Instead, I have discovered one of the most effective live strategies is reviewing student work, both individually and as a group. Most students make similar mistakes and so even looking at my critique of someone else's work adds considerable value. This also has the productive side effect of making the class about them, not me.

This technique also gives me the opportunity to step from behind the curtain and demonstrate the actual work of critique and design to students who are used to seeing the after-effects of my grading without any real idea of how it works. As a consequence, it resembles magic to them. Part of every teacher's job should be demystifying the learning process to students. At the end of the day, getting them to understand and reflect on their own work is actually more important than my own assessments - especially when those assessments seem arbitrary and incomprehensible.

1) Build trust by emphasizing transparency throughout your class.
2) Take stock of your goals for your class but then lead with asking your students what their goals are for the class.
3) Start with your students and then work backwards to get them to buy into the goals of the class.
4) Emphasize student-driven activity during synchronous sessions and let asynchronous activities drive your agenda.

Listening and Learning in an Age of Social Distancing

In March 2020, when we didn't return from Spring Break, I found myself reaching out to several dozen confused, scared students in my three government classes. These were students I had gotten to know during the first six weeks of the semester. Unlike some, I had somewhat of an idea where things were going as early as mid-February and started mapping out what I was going to do. The biggest problem my students have is that many, if not most, of them are first-time college students with no family members to support them through the process. My class emphasizes advanced critical thinking and communication skills, both of which are alien concepts to many.

As soon as I returned from what would be my last trip in a long while, I started the process of reaching out to them via email. My first goal was to reassure them and to check in on their circumstances. My second goal was to point out all of the ways that the class would stay the same and how the skills we had been practicing in person would still be the skills that they would need to succeed in the class. I directed them toward resources and, most importantly, took the time to set up a Zoom meeting with each one of them individually in order to reconnect. I am proud of the fact that I only lost one student that disappeared as a result of the pandemic and remote teaching. That's because my first and only priority was to maintain the conversations that we had established. All of the technology I deployed was fundamentally in service to that goal.

As the pandemic unfolded, I found myself involved in many conversations with faculty and administrators about moving classes online. These conversations rapidly devolved into discussions of the relative merits of various tools. Often these discussions resembled office workers debating the relative merits of plows. They were disconnected from the reality of what was already happening in peoples' classrooms before social isolation took hold. When I started to ask questions about what the intent of specific instructional activities such as lectures, assessment, or discussion was, I was quickly shut down because "no one wants to talk about philosophy now." However, it was precisely the time when we should have been talking about philosophy because it is only when we strip the processes that occur in our learning environments bare that we can grasp at the *correct* tools for both us as teachers and, more importantly, for the learners that depend on us.

Good teachers listen as much as they talk. Diana Laurillard refers to these as "conversational spaces."[12] Teachers need to prioritize tools that enable them to listen and hear because this is what distance robs us of. If the tool is too top-down, your students won't be empowered to talk. If it is too technically difficult, the means of hearing will break down. Communication is the single most important challenge facing anyone who seeks to teach. A good conferencing tool that flattens both the technical and communication curves became an essential tool during the pandemic not because of what it *was* but because of what it *did*. Function should always trump form.

The parts of instruction that we are changing the most are the physical interactions within the classroom. Therefore, it is important to take an honest look at what

---

[12] Laurillard, Ibid

goes on in a stereotypical classroom. Faculty talk at their students. Much of that is misheard or ignored. Better students take notes of information. Often that information is lacking in context, especially if they are simply copying from a whiteboard or PowerPoint slide. In some courses communication doesn't go much further than that. Students may ask for some points of clarification (many don't) and try to make sense out of the information coming at them but that's about the extent of the conversation going on. This is fairly easy to replicate online. Just post notes or PowerPoints slides. Answer questions via email or chat and you're pretty much done. Because of technical challenges and tool limitations, there are a lot of online courses that never go much further than this basic modality.

Those faculty who think deeply about what's going on in the classroom environment realize that this is far from sufficient. One step further would be to engage in the Socratic method with extensive questioning and feedback about student attention and mental engagement within the class. Socratic method is much harder to replicate online because much of its essential feedback is dependent on live, synchronous interactions with students. Watching a video of a Socratic interchange would merely form a more confusing version of a straight lecture paradigm and, arguably, would be more confusing for those not present synchronously. Also, the element of body language and performance inherent in this method is inevitably muted, if not lost entirely, online. There are a number of tools available to facilitate this kind of instruction such as clickers and other electronic feedback mechanisms. None of them, however, overcome the kind of "social distancing" that limits the execution of this approach remotely. Also, it's a lot easier to hide in the back of the online "classroom" and be "present" without being mentally present in the discussion.

Many tools in the learning management system are designed to facilitate these kinds of instruction. They imply a power structure where the instructor is at the front and the class should follow along as best as they can. Some tools may be useful for making that path easier, but the basic communications modality is the same. The more you go down this path, the more complex the tools become. Communication should not be complex. It is a fragile flower, easily broken. Moving thousands of classes online in a time of stress for both instructor and student risks a lot of breakage. Making things more complex with technological tools only exacerbates the danger here.

Another approach would be to back off and consider how *effective* communication occurs between faculty and instructor. For one thing, I walk around the classroom instead of positioning myself in the front. This is a basic technique for making sure even those students who are trying to hide will not be able to do as we engage in class discussion. Conversations like this cannot be replicated in a series of disconnected posts on a discussion board. It is a dynamic interchange which the instructor steers but does not always control. The controlling factor is the students' capacity to absorb information flows in the classroom, not how much material I have to get through. Adjustments are made. Putting information online has the advantage of persistence but we completely lose the spontaneous conversational aspect so critical for the learning process, particularly among students who lack the skills to teach themselves. Start with this problem set and work forward from there.

We are fortunate at this technological junction to have relatively sophisticated videoconferencing capabilities to complement whatever asynchronous capabilities we have developed online. Live conversations offer the only way to achieve immediate feedback and conversation. Set up properly, they can also bring the student to the fore. The best platforms are also technically easy to navigate because they were designed to be used by nontechnical business users on a regular basis. They flatten interactions if they are designed for collaboration over and above presentation/lecture. In an environment where the vast majority of faculty and students have never operated in this way before, this is an obvious tool to grasp for. It most closely mirrors interactions on the classroom level. It requires minimal setup and adaptation from what is going on in the classroom and can work to lessen the distance between teacher and student when distance will be the biggest challenge to overcome. Focusing on other tools risks creating lots of noise in a confusing environment. This is not the best strategy for communication.

Right now, everyone is floating in an atomized soup. Regular bearings are lost in the fog of uncertainty but are coupled with a desire to move forward beyond the immediate crisis. Finding our way back to the basics of what we've always tried to do in the classroom and matching the appropriate tools with the task is critical to the success of that effort. If anything, there are too many tools available to us in this environment. This can be overwhelming. Best to keep it simple, go and grab your favorite hammer or screwdriver, and see if it will do the job in front of you. Don't worry about the rest. Above all, listen to your students. They need to hear your voice clearly now more than ever and you need to hear theirs in order to be understood. That much will never change.

Diana Laurillard's Framework for Understanding How Pedagogical Toolsets Shape Learning

There are many different ways that we teach and learn. Most faculty pursue multiple modalities of instruction over the course of the semester, or even class meeting. To understand what kind of learning environment we are creating, we must first start with our own actions as teachers. It is only when we deconstruct various teaching strategies that we can understand how these approaches are constrained by different technologies and learning spaces. In 2002, Diana Laurillard published *Rethinking University Teaching* in which she developed her "conversational framework"[13] that describes the various ways in which students, teachers, and peers interact to construct effective learning experiences.

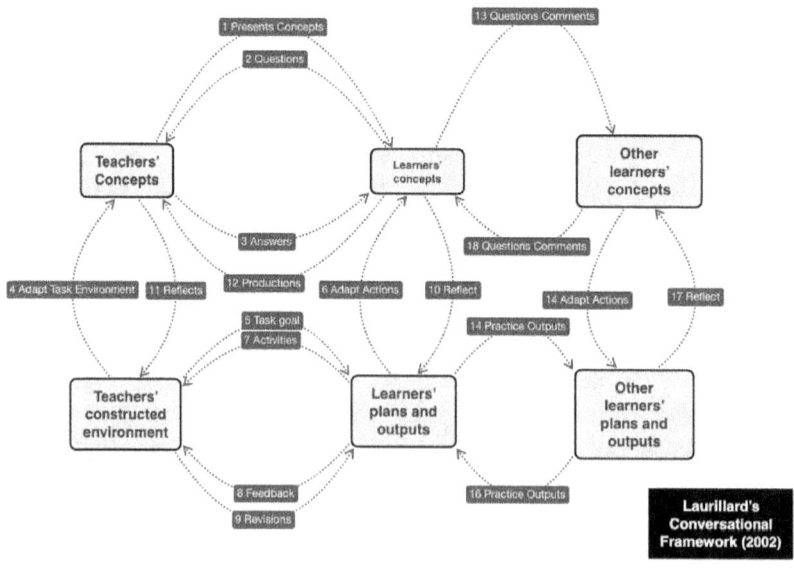

---

[13] Routledge, 2002

This framework is designed to be used to analyze tools and strategies for effective teaching. However, it can also be used to deconstruct and understand different approaches to teaching in the classroom. In a later article, Laurillard defines four instructional modes: Instructionism, Constructionism, Socio-Cultural Learning, and Collaborative Learning. I have adapted her typology here as a mechanism for analyzing pedagogical practices and, ultimately, our analysis of tools.[14]

---

[14] *Typology and images from Laurillard, Diana, "The Pedagogical Challenges to Collaborative Technologies,"* Computer-Supported Collaborative Learning, 2009/4, pp. 7-8)

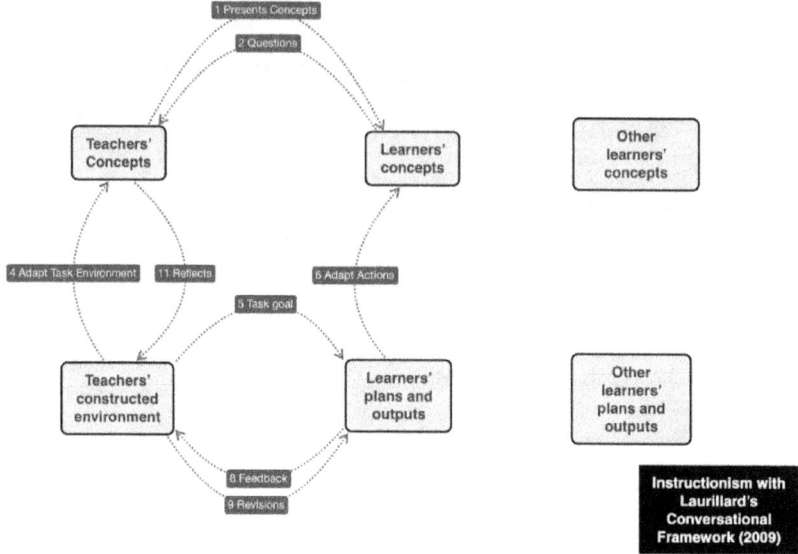

Instructionism – The organization of instruction is the most important factor in the Instructionist approach to teaching and learning. It prioritizes the presentation of material, its testing, and predictable outcomes measurement. Instruction is then adapted based on those predictable outcome measures. The focus in this pedagogical method is on the instructor's ability to present material and test based on said material and typically technology will be instructor-focused in that context.

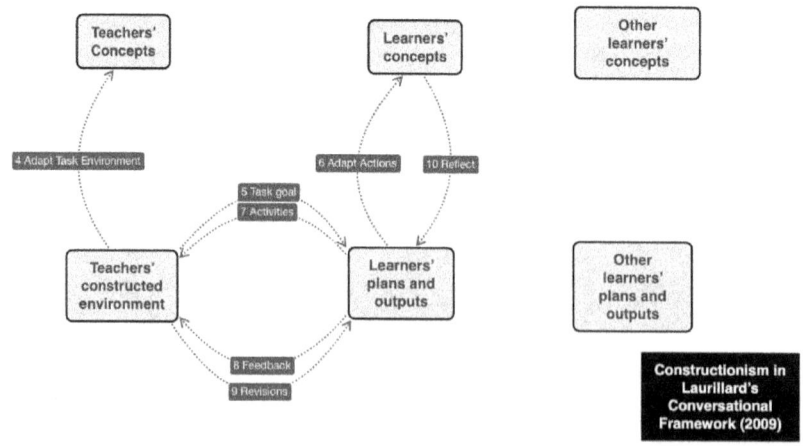

Constructionism – Seymour Papert and Idit Harel coined the term "constructionism" to mean internal self-directed construction of knowledge patterns.[15] This is a learner-focused, often self-directed exploration of learning. The main role of the instructor is to provide the task, provide the necessary technology, and facilitate corrections along the way. This approach to teaching and learning is very hands-on and student-driven and requires technologies that support that approach.

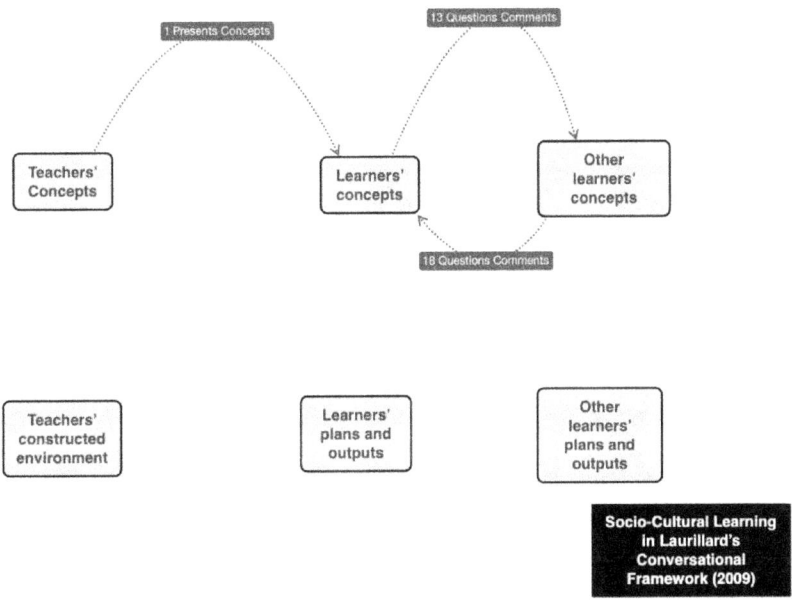

Socio-Cultural Learning in Laurillard's Conversational Framework (2009)

Socio-Cultural Learning – Socio-cultural learning is derived from the concept that learning is a process of conversations, particularly with peers who help each other overcome conceptual challenges. In the early 1930s Russian educational researcher L.S. Vygotsky developed the idea of the **Zone of Proximal Development** to illustrate

---

[15] Papert, Seymour and Idit Harel, *Constructionism*, Ablex Publishing, 1991

the scaffolding of challenges that teachers provide to students as they collectively work their way through the learning journey.[16] Socio-cultural learning is extremely dependent on communications toolsets, particularly those which facilitate group discussions.

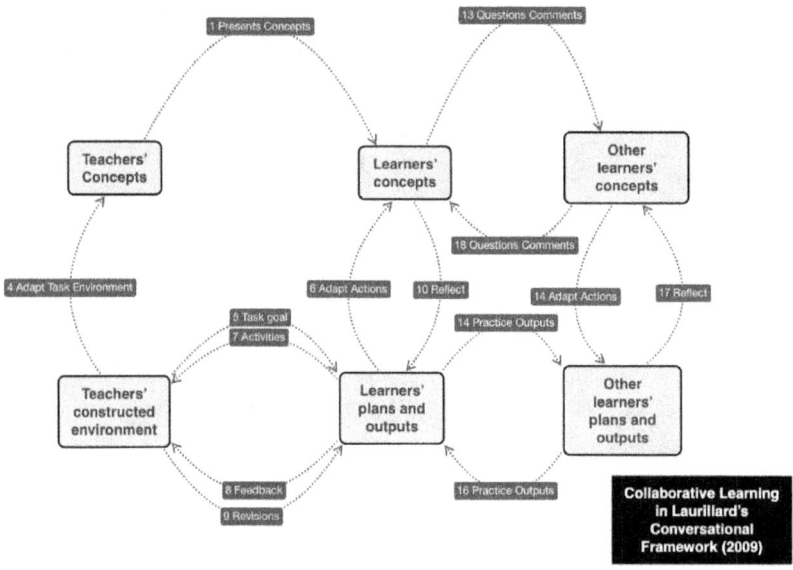

Collaborative Learning – combines many of the elements of the preceding two approaches to teaching and learning. It is still very much a student-centered approach to learning, but it instead theorizes that it is through a combination of peer group learning and practical challenges that learning can be accelerated. It therefore requires toolsets that support both self-constructed learning and easy communication among the students.

Laurillard's frameworks give us a graphical way of looking at these four approaches to the processes of teaching and learning. Most teachers practice all of these

---

[16] L. S. Vygotsky, *Mind in Society: The Development of Higher Psychological Processes*, Boston, Harvard University Press, 1978, pp. 84-91

approaches to a greater or lesser degree over the course of the semester or even within the context of a single lesson.

Going digital requires that we deconstruct what we are doing at any given point in order to align our teaching effectively with the array of tools now available to us. Laurillard's Framework gives us a set of interactions that we can use to design hybrid instruction (and all instruction is "hybrid" at some level) to align as closely as possible with the needs of the individual student's learning journey. Which parts of instruction are most effective in a structured environment such as a classroom or live videoconference? Which parts of instruction are better suited to asynchronous interactions? What kinds of tools foster interaction and collaboration necessary for social and collaborative learning? What new avenues are opened for learners to construct knowledge by the implementation of new technologies such as MakerSpaces or XR? Understanding the framework of learning is critical to understanding the tools we discussed in Chapter 1 but it is also critical to overcoming some of the systemic challenges imposed on us by the industrial education system. How we are heard is more essential to the success of our students than what we say.

Chapter 3
The Currency of Teaching

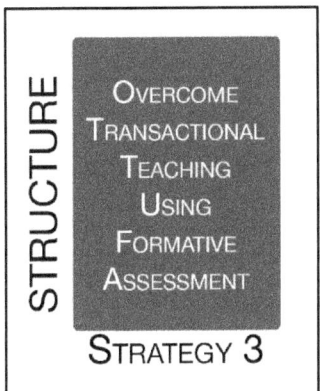

Learning is a process of iterative failure. This process is dependent on an ability to move through the system, see a point to the exercises being assigned, and connecting those to a larger learning goal. Rank ordering students based on their progress through this process is counter-productive to long-term outcomes. Many of our class grading systems are based on doing precisely that, leading to what I call "transactional teaching" where grades become nothing more than an artificial currency, signifying no real value whatsoever. According to T.J Crook's 30-year old review of assessment strategies, "[M]any students aimed to plan their study with the primary goal of performing well on course examinations and other evaluation tasks. Unfortunately, the students often saw this goal as conflicting with the more fundamental goal of gaining a deep and enduring grasp of the subject."[17] There is little evidence that this has changed in the intervening decades; we continue to willfully ignore the underlying problems of making school a transactional process.

Moving instruction online only exacerbates this problem because it undermines whatever interpersonal strategies that you might have employed to mitigate early failures in class. The strategy is pretty simple even though its execution can be logistically complex. Take a moment to assess (pun intended) the outcomes you are trying to measure, not just in content but also in the skills necessary to process content, and ask yourself if your students can achieve a higher-order outcome by shifting the nature of their assessment to a different level. Use this assessment to design precise tasks whose completion demonstrates a level of mastery (or not). Completing these tasks results in an unambiguous result that builds towards a final class goal. Achievement of that class goal can then be assessed in a more summative manner.

My class can be described as a set of building blocks toward a final goal. In order to achieve this, I use Emily Wray's RISE model to design my assignments based on the level of work that I'm expecting the student to achieve.[18] Wray's schema is essentially a simplified version of Bloom's taxonomy. At the base level, students are expected to *Reflect* on the work of others. At the second level, they are expected to bring work to the conversation from outside in a process of *Inquiry*. At the third level, they are expected to critically assess and engage with the work of their peers and *Suggest* stronger ways of expressing those

---

[17] Crook, Terence J, "The Impact of Classroom Evaluation Practices on Students." *Review of Educational Research*, 58.4 (Winter 1988), p. 445
[18] risemodel.com

ideas. Finally, they create their own versions of ideas by *Elevating* their work. With college students I can generally start at the Inquiry level. I task them with seeking out new information on a topic that interests them and show them how to evaluate the quality and biases of the sources they bring to the table. I use this to build toward products that gradually incorporate Elevate elements. As a capstone to the class, I require my students to produce a final portfolio that measures their ability to process and communicate information about government. In this way, students *construct* knowledge themselves.[19] On a skills level, the difficulty builds up gradually through a deliberate strategy based on Zones of Proximal Development.[20] Those students who diligently work toward that task and have iterated their activities enough through a formative assessment process tend to operate at a higher level than the one they entered the class with.

With the final portfolio I am less concerned about the comprehensiveness of their content mastery than I am in their ability to be able to find relevant information, analyze it, and use it to advocate for an issue that matters to them. This is also a design choice. As this website is their own creation and on their choice of platform, it also creates opportunities for active learning as we work together to improve what they are trying to say, how they are trying to say it, and how this is ultimately presented. It is a lasting artifact of their work in the class. It is a form of assessment with meaning. And it is the only part of the class that I rank order assess qualitatively. In the spirit of transparency, however, I work hard all semester long to give students qualitative feedback on their formative assignments and

---

[19] Papert and Harel
[20] Vygotsky

there are clear linkages between work assessed in this manner and the capstone assignment.

1) Work backwards from the "ends" of your class instead of forwards from the beginning.
2) Create assignments that demonstrate competency by doing rather than judgement from on high - especially early in the course.
3) Incorporate specific activities that force students to look backwards at their own (and their peers') work.

Understanding and Countering Transactional Teaching

It's the first day of class (or the last day before the drop) and a student comes up to me and asks: "How do I pass this class?" It's almost never, "What can I learn in the class," or "How can this class help me understand the world a bit better?" I entered teaching thinking that it was about the latter two questions because that's how I have always approached learning. I get this from my mother. As a girl growing up postwar Germany, she was routed in an "appropriate" direction and denied the chance for higher education in part because she was a girl and in part because my grandmother did not advocate for her. When she married my father and moved to the United States, she enrolled in college in her 40s and graduated Summa Cum Laude six years later; not because she was trying to advance some sort of career, but because she wanted to know more. I have had to explain to her time and time again how most of my students approach education and that it has very little to do with actual learning. Learning happens by accident for most (including my own children), the rest is entirely transactional in nature and this is incredibly destructive to the mission that we see ourselves on as educators.

At the end of the day, I'm nothing more than a currency manipulator. I control an entire economy all by myself. I sit on rewards and incentives and have more control over their distribution than even the most repressive regimes in history. I am a teacher.

My society of students actively understand this and, like every repressed society, they act out. Instead of looking to the intrinsic benefits that learning can bring to them they focus most of their energy on currying favor with the dictator. If there was a way to trade currency, I am sure they would do so because in the end it has a little real short-term value to them. Like the process of hyperinflation, this cheapens the entire process and encourages them to hoard worthless currency with little regard to what it actually earns them.

As most dictators discover, outside of the torture chamber, they have very little real power over their societies. The society will develop its own transactional economy. In the classroom this is a very stilted economy because the market is dead. There is no possibility for trade and therefore whatever motivation there is to create communities in order to maximize individual gain is at best an abstract concept. It is paradoxical in the extreme to bribe people to collectivize. Collaborative behavior is fundamentally intrinsic. Extrinsic motivators to engage in group behavior quickly turn to farce.

It is a rare student indeed that transcends this debasing marketplace. The dictator treasures those students because they are the only thing that drives society forward. However, the dictator has no control over how many of those students he receives or whether they have any sort of impact on the larger society. The profit-maximizing majorities tend to overwhelm any intrinsic activity.

One strategy I have attempted for several years now is to minimize the incentives around any one given activity and, furthermore, to design those activities to force students to engage in the kind of intrinsic behaviors that I am seeking. Taken from the gaming world where the bigger the monster you slay, the greater the reward, this approach seeks to "level up" students through the completion of specific tasks. I liken it to paying people to go to the gym.

The problem with that strategy is that people will do the minimum amount of workout and won't spend a second longer at the gym than they are getting paid to do. Furthermore, they are far less likely to return after the incentive program is over. For example, I require my students to submit six sources to build into the foundation of their research in my class. They never submit 8. They almost never go back after the assignment and augment this trove of information. Qualitatively, they just check the box regardless of the value the source might or might not have for them in the future.

As a dictator I am powerless to walk away from this because the larger inter-course system requires it of me. I am required to submit my periodic bounty to a higher power at the end of the reporting period and in many systems I, myself, am rewarded based on the richness of my bounty. Again, this incentivizes cheating the system; this time by those who control their own economies. In some systems the ability to engage in this form of economic cheating is supposedly mitigated by external economies such as standardized testing regimes. This has all of the hallmarks of colonialism with all of the pernicious side-effects of undermining or destroying whatever local civic culture remains. Production declines and the economic actors are further disincentivized to act in their own interests and instead turn their attention to the desires of the master, whether that be the local dictator or the repressive world government.

This a poor environment for learning and yet, in most classes, learning takes place despite these disincentives. The critical missing element: conversations with someone who is deeply committed to the project of learning. You see, most successful (benevolent) dictators wear two hats. One of them requires them to extract benefits from their economies. Toilets still need to be cleaned, assembly lines manned, and goods delivered. But this is not the makings of a vibrant society. The other hat requires an explicit nurturing of culture for life is not measured in acquisition. It is measured in joy. Transactional economies stagnate creatively in the absence of a larger culture. Trying to transactionalize creativity results in lots of Hollywood sequels. Any art is incidental to the process.

And herein lies the trap of online learning. Computers make it easy to engage in transactional learning. They tabulate, communicate scores, and automate transactions far more efficiently than we are able to do with pencil and paper or their equivalents. Where the factors of distance and time (and a tendency to exploit the efficiencies of them to maximize class sizes) fail is in making authentic conversations possible.

Some students can easily waltz through my class, merrily collecting the points I leave along the way. That just means that they have already mastered the fundamentals of the mental gymnastics I'm asking them to perform. As a consequence, they learn very little. The best I can hope to do is irritate them around the edges with points laced with unobtanium. Many of those students, however, also recognize those incentives as unnecessary for their ultimate grade and ignore them. For them, moving online has little impact on outcomes.

Most students, however, struggle to grasp the connections I'm trying to form in my class. It is in that connective tissue, not the tasks themselves, that 80% of the learning takes place. When those conversations do not take place, learning becomes a dead, transactional space. Students implicitly recognize this even as they are forced to behave like market-driven rats, and it is here that I am convinced much of their dissatisfaction with the online learning experience occurs.

There is no substitute for the benevolent dictator in these audiences and turning interactions into a ping-pong match of asynchronous messaging is not generally very productive. One strategy I employ is to force students to review their work with me in person. I can do more actual teaching in 15 minutes of conversation than in any assessment, commentary, or email exchange. During those 15 minutes I do specific exercises getting them to apply the transactionally-acquired content in various ways. One method I have discovered recently has been the application of the Toulmin Method to get them to dissect the arguments they are trying to make in their design challenges. It's impossible to turn these kinds of activities into transactions, but by giving them new keys to unlock their points in subsequent work, I get them to engage in a tertiary activity and learn "by accident" how to construct argumentation but it requires my active intervention and engagement.[21]

---

[21] For more on the Toulmin Method see https://owl.purdue.edu/owl/general_writing/academic_writing/historical_perspectives_on_argumentation/toulmin_argument.html

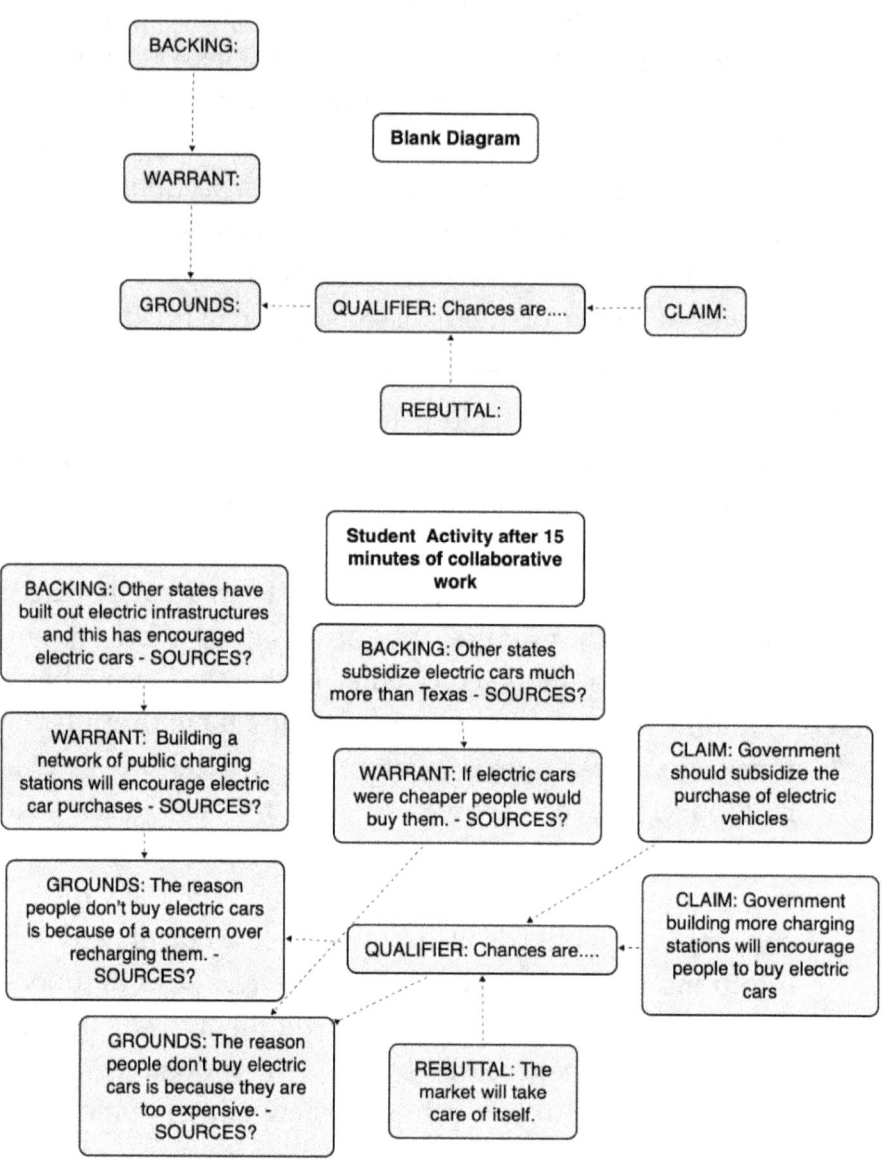

Example of a student exercise using the Toulmin Method to dissect arguments.

It is the conversations that make our cruel, misshapen, market-driven courses bearable. Therefore, the first priority of any international (inter-coursal) power is to recognize the pernicious effects of an incentive-driven economy and to prioritize spaces for conversation as it adapts to the exigencies of distanced teaching. Traditional teaching often puts us too far away from true learning; we should not let crisis tip us into the academic abyss.

What are the resources in this economy? It is easy to think that the dictator/teacher/currency manipulator holds all of the resource cards. In truth, the currency holds little value. The true value in this economy is the labor of its participants. If the labor is directed well, it may actually produce a tangible product that also holds value. However, the real value underlying all of this effort is the intrinsic growth of the labor force. My objectives as a teacher are to foster skill and knowledge. But these are wants on my part that are not necessarily intrinsically reflected in my labor force. The only currency that matters to most of my students is the one that's reflected in the end game. All of the other transactions merely increase or decrease their stress levels associated with achieving their intended outcomes and have little to do with actual learning. Most of my efforts lie in fostering intrinsic efforts that are often at odds with their priorities. Therefore, all of my assignments are focused squarely on learning by doing with the implicit hope that, through repetition and the nature of their efforts, they will grow. If I do this right, they will take something with them that is not reflected on their transcript. However, the means by which I have to carry it out work against that.

Therein lies the fundamental challenge of transactional teaching. We are forced into a situation where we have to exchange worthless currency for meaningful product. The most effective means of doing this is to treat the currency as if it were truly worthless or only had ephemeral value, like the points in a game that are cashed in at the end for a more tangible prize. By keeping your students firmly focused on the tangible prize at the end and emphasizing the importance of learning by doing, the process is redirected toward the nurturing of personal growth. Ideally, we will eventually get rid of the false economy of grades in favor of more authentic assessment.[22] However, that is a project of decades. In the meantime, we must recognize the pernicious impact transactional teaching has on our efforts to stimulate true learning in our students and recognize that grades do not represent the authentic currency of learning, conversations do.

---

[22] "Thinking Backwards: A Knowledge Network for the 21st Century" at http://www.ideaspaces.net/thinking-backward/

PART II
Teaching and Learning Holistically
to Harness Time and Space

- *Create Space for Understanding*
- *Reflect on Practice*
- *Seize Unexpected Digital Opportunities*

Chapter 4

Creating Informal Spaces to Support Atomized Learning

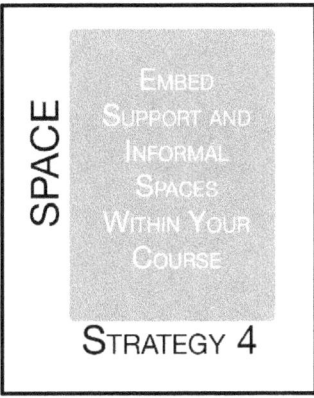

The STAC Model (Stickiness-Toolsets-Adjacencies-Community) was originally designed as a guide to the design of physical spaces in a shifting digital environment. Most of us don't have that measure of control over the design of the physical spaces where we have to teach. This is wrong and something I've been seeking to rectify for years in my involvement in the design of various physical spaces in both K12 and higher education. However, what distinguishes the STAC Model is that, like the Teaching Toolset Triangle, it is based on a set of principles about teaching and learning, conversational spaces, and technology, not on any set of architectural or physical principles. That means its basic concepts are just as applicable to digital environments as they are to physical ones. Distance and time may provide more challenges to informal interactions among students, but the benefits of such interaction don't change, nor does human behavior. The basic principles of the STAC Model are:

1) Give students ownership over their informal learning spaces
2) Give students empowering tools that promote sharing and collaboration
3) Provide human support in one or more of
   - Library services (information support)
   - Tutoring (learning skills support)
   - Making (design support)
   - Counseling (mental support)
4) Create connections to larger learning universes such as other institutions of learning or community resources

These resources should be front and center in any environment as students may not realize (or be willing to admit) that they need help. Resources may therefore appear irrelevant and unrelated to any given classes they are taking.

As teachers, we have some control over this because, in many ways, we have more control over these spatial challenges in digital environments than in physical ones. Teachers cannot change how their classes are situated within physical structures, nor do they have much control over how informal environments are situated around it. Therefore, we feel like we can put this problem out of our minds as unsolvable.

In a digital world, however, these challenges are not unsolvable. Instead of worrying about where your class is located with regards to these important supporting services, you can *bring these elements into your class digitally*. I have already implemented the first two elements of the STAC Model into my course shell. First, front and center on my class home page, I have created a Learning Commons which is explicitly an area where students have access to a range of communication tools where they can initiate asynchronous communications by creating their own Discussion topics, synchronous text communications through Chat, and synchronous video connections via a Conference tool. These are all grouped together so that they can be easily found and are one of the first things students see when they open the course.

I have also taken tentative steps to integrate support services into the class. Instead of flinging students out onto the college website to contact the library for assistance, I have added a librarian into the class as a Teaching Assistant. In addition to having her own page, she does scheduled live services for the students (which are recorded as well) and is available for consultations. I don't have to worry about where the administration decided to locate the library. I've moved it into my classroom. This is a digital opportunity.

While I have not done this myself yet, our digital shift has made it possible to bring people into your class from anywhere in the world. Your videoconferencing solution doesn't care whether the participants are a mile away from you or in another country. If you are a high school teacher and want to bring in a professor from a distant college or university to inspire your students to pursue studies in your area there are few barriers to making this happen, to cite just one such opportunity. People applying principles from your teaching to real world opportunities can be brought into your virtual "classroom" without the usual concerns around travel or building access, to cite another.

The digital world separates us in distance and time and there is sometimes no substitute for being in a room together and working through a set of challenges. However, this is not an either-or proposition. It is my hope that many of the unexpected opportunities that have resulted from our enforced isolation will carry over once the pandemic is a memory. Informal learning happens wherever students gather. The media really doesn't matter in the end as it is the community that inspires deep and lasting learning.

1) Informal spaces should not be afterthoughts in learning design. Create space for the informal wherever you can.
2) Imagine informal spaces divorced from the strictures of space and time.
3) Make teaching a team activity by embedding people resources in your class.
4) Actively create student-centered learning spaces in your class based on blank canvases instead of fixed notions of what the spaces were designed for.

Introducing the STAC Model (Stickiness-Toolsets-Adjacencies-Community)

In 2012 I was placed in charge of redesigning two floors of an office building into a community college campus. It was an odd-shaped building and, as usual, we did not have enough money to realize the dreams of the collaborative team that imagined the use of the spaces. The result, however, was an accidental serendipity. It turned out that classrooms were more expensive than informal spaces and the odd shape the building created all of these weirdly shaped nooks and crannies. My team leaned into that. We started thinking about them as connective tissue and created lots of pods of with tables and seating for students to work. I advocated for hanging whiteboards in strategic places so that students would have a work surface. Communal whiteboards were resisted by some because they assumed that they would be abused, and we would find lewd pictures scrawled across them.

After the construction was complete, I moved my offices into the new area and watched with interest what would happen when the students were let loose in the new areas. The whiteboards were immediately covered with mathematical formulas and charts. The most subversive thing I saw was someone drawing a period with an arrow pointing at it with the label, "the point." Empowering these students with these accidental spaces changed the entire atmosphere of the campus and created unexpected zones of learning and community.

Every environment tells a story to its inhabitants. The story can be one of control or one of empowerment. While both physical and online spaces are sometimes radically adapted to the needs of their human inhabitants, their design sets a tone for the kinds of activity that can occur within them. In a controlled classroom environment, a dynamic teacher can overcome some of the limitations of the instructional space (although arguably he or she shouldn't have to). In informal environments this is not really possible. Students will walk with their feet if the space doesn't meet their needs. Informal spaces are where students see learning happening. Better students model behavior to peers who aren't used to self-directed learning and productively shift learning cultures.

If designed properly, a student-centric empowered learning space can become a crucial set of tools for facilitating learning throughout the college, school, or online program. In an era when online learning has become such an important modality, informal spaces become even more critical to success. For hybrid students a well-designed campus space can provide a critical learning anchor for their online activity. Taking this to another level, the creation of wholly online student informal environments could help bridge the engagement gap that is a serious impediment to effective online learning.

At the beginnings of online learning, Diana Laurillard engaged in a deconstruction of teaching and learning in an attempt to construct technological environments that would augment teaching and learning. Obviously, online environments are technological environments, but properly designed physical environments are also interfaces with technology and should follow the same principles. All should be "productive" environments, which Laurillard describes as including "microworlds, productive tools, and modelling environments" in which the learner can "build something," "engage with the subject," and "learn how to represent these relationships in some general formalism."[23] All informal learning environments, both online and in person, should aspire to be productive environments. Students will be drawn to them and they are likely to form a critical backbone for their educational journeys. Environments designed in this way have the potential to transform a billboard of information into a community of learning.

Informal spaces should therefore be viewed as a set of learning tools. The STAC Model is designed to prioritize "productive" engagement and align college services to support this kind of engagement. The four elements of the STAC model are, *Stickiness, Toolsets, Adjacencies, and Community Engagement*. Together, they are designed to create an environment that keeps students in the space and interacting with other students while exposing them to new opportunities and resources designed to elicit curiosity and creativity.

The Holy Grail of informal learning spaces is the achievement of true peer learning environments. There is ample evidence to indicate that if you can get the students to pull together toward their learning goals that outcomes will dramatically improve.[24] Residential campuses have a distinct advantage in this area because the number of opportunities for social interaction on campus grow exponentially when students also live there. Conversely, non-residential campuses often struggle with student interaction and, ironically, community-building, because students tend to "visit" campus and then return to their

---

[23] Laurillard 2003, p. 171
[24] Astin 1991

"real" lives. Online "campuses" face perhaps the greatest challenges in this regard because of their technology design and the remoteness of the student experience.

Anything that keeps students interacting with peers longer has been shown to improve learning outcomes. As Alexander Astin wrote over a quarter century ago, "The single most powerful source of influence on the undergraduate student's academic and personal development is the peer group. In particular, we found that the amount of interaction among peers has far-reaching effects on nearly all areas of student learning and development."[25] David Zandvliet notes, "A review of the eco-psychological literature similarly reveals a focus on interpersonal and community factors that reflect value, fairness, respect, and collaboration. This emphasis indicates the importance of community for environmental learning at both the micro and macro levels."[26] The design and integration of informal spaces into the overall learning mission of the institution is therefore critical.

The first level of the STAC model is designed to support student-centric needs *now* and is driven by the goal of facilitating productive peer interaction. The second level of the STAC Model represents the supporting elements that the college provides to expose students to *new* opportunities and support. However, if the needs of the first level are compromised by the second, the overall effectiveness of the space will be substantially undermined. If students find access to the spaces to be unreliable places to gather, they are far less likely to stick in them.

---

[25] Ibid
[26] Zandvliet 2012, p. 127

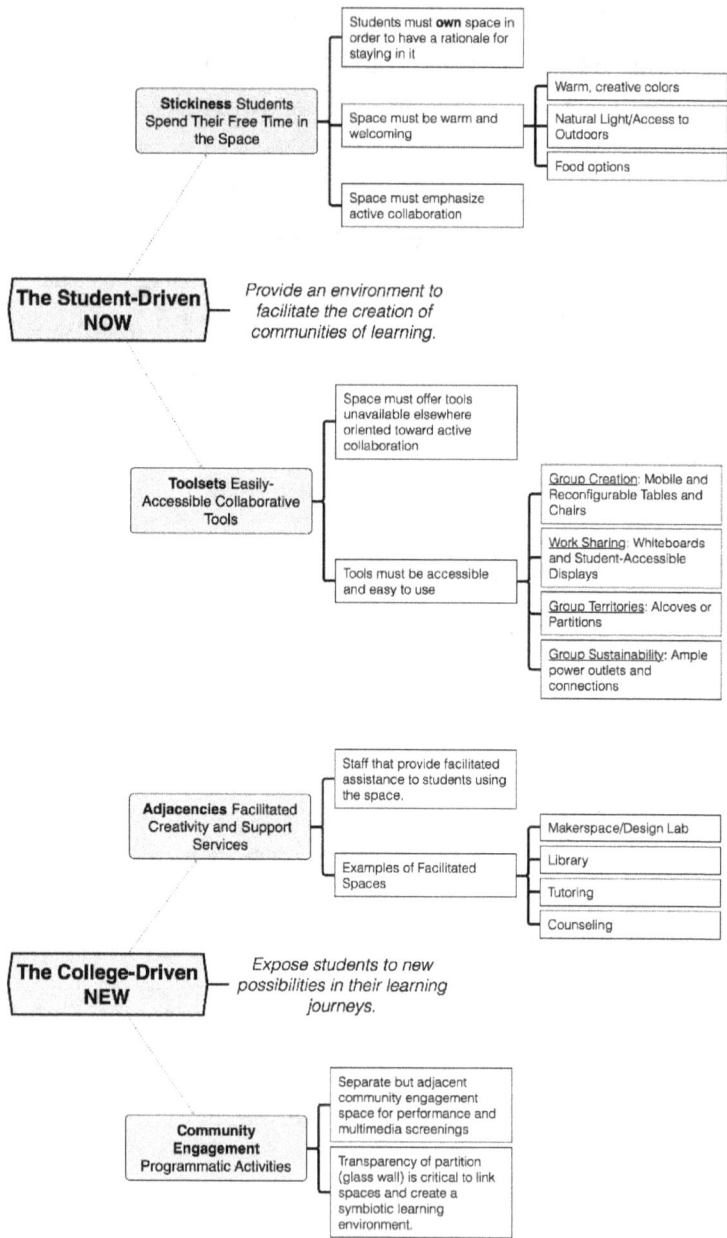

Designing Physical Spaces Using the STAC Model

Level 1 – The Student-Driven NOW

The fundamental rule of productive spaces is that they need to provide an environment that is driven by the students first and foremost. If the students are deprived of agency, they are unlikely to persist in the space and/or find alternatives at the first possible opportunity. The two basic levels of the STAC model are therefore fundamental to the success of any productive space because they provide a rationale for being in the space in the first place and, more importantly, a rationale for coming into the space and returning to it whenever possible. Without these preconditions any activities related to the second level will have to first overcome the burden of creating an audience before anything programmatically new can even begin. These are not facilitated spaces. They are *facilitating* spaces. The second level spaces are where the facilitation occurs. While having a complete suite of services available to students is the ideal, if first level criteria are met, the space can still be productive. Furthermore, second level activities cannot be allowed to impinge on first level functions at the risk of ruining the student-centric logic of the space.

Stickiness: The space needs to provide an environment that is welcoming to students and provides a rationale for them to stay on campus to work and interact with peers. The critical aspect of this is that the students, within the bounds of reasonable safety and maintenance considerations, should be able to reside and reconfigure the space to meet their immediate needs. The space should also accommodate longer term occupancy and provide food services where appropriate. Finally, the décor should reflect these priorities. The best way to get students to congregate is to give this space a "clubhouse" feel, where they know they will find their communities of practice.

Toolsets: The space needs to include easily accessible collaborative tools. These fall into four functional categories:

1) **Group Creation** – Furniture must be mobile and reconfigurable to support a range of group sizes up to 10 people. Tables and chairs on casters that be easily combined to create larger group sets are essential here. Round tables are generally to be avoided because they dictate the size of the group.

2) **Work Sharing** – Whiteboards and student-accessible displays are critical to group functionality. These should also be as mobile as possible throughout the space in order to support different group locations. These tools should also provide a linkage to digital tools such as concept mapping and file repositories.

3) **Group Territories** – Groups need to be able to establish temporary territories where they can segregate themselves from

other groups. There are at least two ways to accomplish this. First, you can use mobile partitions (which could also be writable surfaces like whiteboards) or you can build alcoves into the space where groups can congregate. The second solution is a bit more inflexible and uses up edge space which might be better used to support Adjacencies (below).
4) **Group Sustainability** – There should be ample power outlets and other relevant connections so that group cohesion is not dictated by battery life. WiFi is assumed as well to support access to online resources.

Level 2 – The College-Driven NEW

The second level functions of these spaces are where the institution can make an impact with its own agency. Part of college is exposing students to people and experiences that enrich their skills or views of the world. That is fundamentally what Level 2 spaces are about. More important than the spaces themselves, however, are the people that inhabit those spaces. Some of these are regular staff who can expose students to new ways of learning or entirely new disciplines. These spaces can also act as a conduit to the larger community outside the institution. Using technology, these experiences can even be geographically unbound such as bringing in remote speakers/facilitators via video-conferencing technology.

Adjacencies: Services that support student activity should be located *adjacent* to the space and not in the space itself. These are staffed areas that may have more limited hours than the main space. These spaces provide specialized capabilities and, more importantly, have support staff who can assist students in exploring new things. Transparency is key to linking these spaces to the central hub of informal learning. Some examples of adjacencies are:

1) **Makerspace/Design Lab** – an accessible space for creating physical products that can range from 3D printing to vinyl cutting to laser cutting. This should be a low barrier to entry space that hosts periodic workshops on a variety of topics to include both student requests and staff initiatives.
2) **Library** – the Library should provide information support to the space as well as tools associated with a Digital Media Commons to complement the activities of the Design Lab in the creation of digital products such as videos, websites, etc.
3) **Tutoring** – A series of small rooms should be provided for tutoring support for students. These rooms can be shared with the main space or the library for quiet study when they are not staffed by tutors.

4) **Counseling** – Many students require emotional and guidance support during their educational journeys. Having access to advisors and counselors can often meet critical needs that can often determine success or failure in school.

Community Engagement: This is a key intersectional space that can be used to provide a venue to speakers, films and other kinds of events. In addition to internal initiatives, it should also be used as a key linkage with the outside community in order to expose students to the life of the wider communities in which the school resides (e.g., geographical, academic, professional). Like adjacencies, transparency should be provided to the greatest extent possible so that the space can be visible from the main space without competing with it acoustically. This space should be configured as a large theater-like area with reconfigurable seating, a large display or projector, and some sort of podium/stage for speakers. It should be acoustically insulated from the larger main collaboration area.

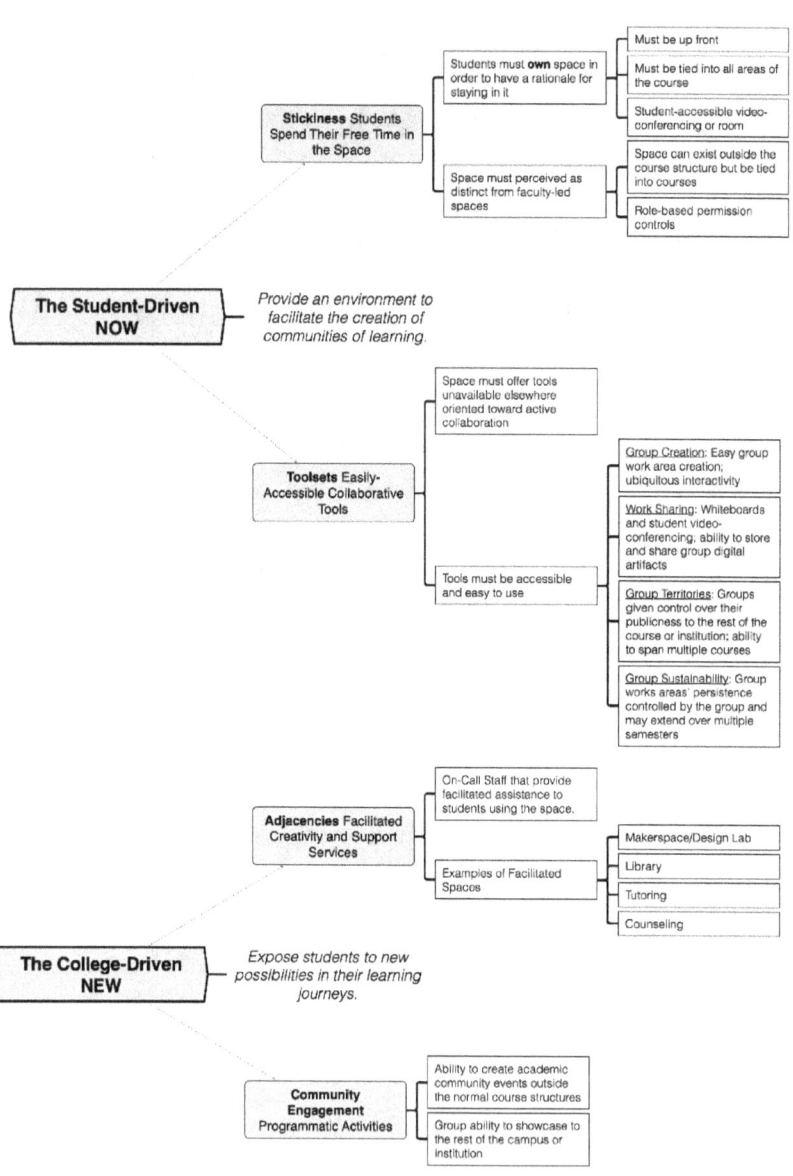

Designing Online Spaces Using the STAC Model

The same basic principles used in designing physical spaces can be applied to online environments. The STAC Model avoids the McLuhanesque mistake that characterizes many online environments by focusing on the underlying *purposes* of any space instead of simply replicating functionalities that might work in a physical environment into a virtual one. Effective learning is universal. Its modalities aren't. If you understand *why* you are designing a space the way that you do, it is possible to create new kinds of online spaces and identify areas of opportunity that augment the human capacity for learning using the tools made available by the disconnection from space and time that online networks offer us.

Level 1 – The Student-Driven NOW

Students have often been viewed with a level of suspicion in online spaces. There seems to be far more discussion of controlling the environment because of fears such as cheating or electronic vandalism than there is of student agency in online environments. It's no accident, therefore, that students often perceive their learning environments as being uninviting places to spend their hours online. The logic for Level 1 spaces remains the same in an online environment even as its realization becomes even more challenging. If we don't want students to log on, go to their class spaces, and do the minimum necessary before logging off, then consideration must be given to designing student-centric spaces that are at least partially under student control.

Stickiness: To the extent possible, students must feel that they have ownership and control over their online congregation spaces.

> 1) Spaces need to be very prominent and accessible throughout any course as this environment will be unexpected to most students.
>
> 2) On-demand videoconferencing or other interactive modalities (think Fortnite without the shooting) can be used to facilitate a "club-like" atmosphere.
>
> 3) Interactivity with outside social media tools foster engagement.

Toolsets: The environment needs to include easily accessible collaborative tools. These fall into four categories:

1) **Group Creation** – Group spaces must be easy to form from a wide variety of areas in the online environment.
2) **Work Sharing** – Groups should have access to a range of shared interactive tools such as digital whiteboards, concept mapping, and student videoconferencing on demand in addition to a mechanism for storing and sharing files.

3) **Group Territories** – Groups need to be able to define their digital territories. This means that they need to be able to control the publicness of their group activities from the rest of the institution (subject to administrator override). Group spaces should also span multiple courses and even be disconnected from any online course registration at all.

4) **Group Sustainability** – Groups should also be able to control the persistence of their online spaces, extending even beyond the bounds of a given semester or even graduation. While limits will probably need to be placed on this capability, there is benefit in extending learning beyond the traditional boundaries of classroom instruction and even to bringing in non-student members such as community members and mentors.

Level 2 – The Institution-Driven NEW

The online environment provides interesting, and, for the most part unexplored, possibilities for experience and support facilitation. With the right tools, staff and faculty could fairly easily devise online experiences for students divorced from the need for a physical infrastructure. Online tutoring and counseling are perhaps the most developed here but other areas have real potential to transform the online student experience.

Adjacencies: Services need to be packaged with the student experience. The key distinguishing element of these elements is the fact that those services are staffed (and consequently may have more limited hours than other spaces within the LMS). There are two ways of doing this. First, as I described in the strategy section of this chapter, these services can be embedded within individual class shells. This is a strategy I used starting in Summer 2020 as part of my pandemic responsive redesigned online classes. Alternatively, these spaces can be placed outside of the sections into the more informal areas of the institutions' online presence. The key factor is that you have to meet the students where they are. Therefore, these spaces need to be accessible from anywhere within the LMS environment and be readily apparent to student users to be effective:

1) **Digital Makerspace** – This would be an interesting concept to explore. The fundamental essence of a Makerspace is creating accessible tools and human interactions centered around making things rather than consuming them. Perhaps this could be a hackerspace with digital programming tools that allow students to build coded creations rather than physical artifacts. Another possible model for this would be to create an online design studio with remote 3D printing where students could go into a lab and pick up their product at their convenience. In either case, the staff should be

well-versed in the design process and should offer periodic workshops in design and prototyping as they would in a physical space.

2) **Library** – The Library staff should provide information support via videoconferencing to the environment. Media tools associated with a Digital Media Commons can complement the activities of the Digital Makerspace in the creation of digital products such as videos and websites. The staff would give periodic synchronous and asynchronous workshops on strategies for effective research and communication.

3) **Tutoring** – Online tutoring services are a critical part of the support package. Synchronous and asynchronous modes should both be supported in this area. This would also be a logical place for workshops on student success strategies.

4) **Counseling** – In a physical environment, it makes sense to place counseling services (ADA, course planning, and psychological) in a separate area, but online there is a logic to proximity since students are more likely to struggle in finding these kinds of resources and privacy is defined much differently if physical proximity is a non-issue. As such, counseling and related student services need to be digitally "adjacent" to all areas of the

online learning environment in order for them to be apparent to the student users.

Community Engagement: All of these online environments need to have a built-in tool to create online events where speakers and other events can be broadcast to the larger community rather within the "walls" of a single course. These tools must be easily accessible and ubiquitous to administrators and faculty wishing to reach out to the larger community. This is actually easier in an online environment as speakers can be remote and the usual physical limitations of room sizes can be eliminated altogether (although organizers should still have the ability to manage group sizes for interactive reasons). Many institutions and organizations exploited this to great effectiveness during the pandemic of 2020, giving professionals and students alike access to a universe of experts and speakers that otherwise would have been inaccessible for a variety of reasons.

Designing Environments that Create Community

By drilling down to basic principles of what the environment is intended to provide, we can establish a set of priorities centered on student empowerment and engagement. At a minimum, any effective informal space must cover the individual needs of students in the STAC Model (Stickiness and Toolsets) to create an environment where students will willingly congregate. Most of the cost and complexity of this space is associated with institutional-level learning support activities (Adjacencies and Community Engagement).

Finally, and most importantly, STAC must form the basis for the management of the environments, both online and in-person. Environments can facilitate desired activities. They do not in themselves create those activities. They must be managed according to the priorities of the STAC Model giving student empowerment and access to tools priority over all other activities in the space. Informal spaces are by their very nature fragile environments, often occupied by students who are unsure of how to make maximum use of them. Attempts to "control" these spaces can easily disrupt these tentative explorations of what it means to be a lifelong learner and diminish the overall dynamic of the campus or online platform as an effective learning environment. This is not the story we want our learning spaces to tell.

Chapter 5

Tuning Instruction for a Digital World

In a physical classroom, my greatest enemy was almost always the clock. As teachers, we are always dealing with time. It is the truly scarce aspect of instruction. We must confront a limited attention span on both the part of the teacher and student. At the same time, we are faced with significant content expectations that either we or our institutions have for our classes.

One of the hardest things to do as we leap from class to class and from semester to semester is to shake up our habits and do a critical appraisal of how we are getting through our teaching days, weeks, and semesters. We need to reimagine what it means to spend time on tasks. The Digital Age gives us the opportunity to do so.

I have never found time-based expectations to be in alignment with outcomes. I used to blame myself for this reality but in the end, I recognized that there were limits to what my students could absorb within a given timeframe. A number of years back, I came to the realization that the priority of my class should not be the amount of content that the students were able to absorb but, rather, their skills and abilities to absorb that content when they were ready to, even if that moment occurred long after the course was over. Instead of giving them a bunch of content to process, I give them a process with which to process content. This way, they were actually using the content rather than simply absorbing it, to be excreted only on test day. My class goals are therefore centered on what I want them to be able to do rather than what they know. Skills are temporally evergreen.

Digital both compresses and stretches our notions of time. On the one hand, its ability to create persistent objects means that for those kinds of content that are evergreen, time is infinite. This applies to both student work and teacher content. Bending time presents us with a digital opportunity. First, we can push a lot of our content into an asynchronous format where students can go back and review it when they need it, not just when you are available to deliver it. I have always said that there is no pedagogical logic to having English from 10-11 and Government from 11-12; students don't learn on a schedule. If a learning moment comes to a student out of sync with the artificial schedule that has been laid out for them, then it is at best marginalized or, at worst, discarded altogether. Also, having evergreen student content means that you can go back and look at the progression of their work with them. Assuming you have them working in public, you can do this collectively. Rarely in our classes do we have time for true reflection on past work even though this is absolutely critical for learning and growth.

On the flip side, synchronous moments become rarer and more compressed. In completely asynchronous courses it may be impossible to get all the students together at the same time and place. As we discussed in the last chapter, separation of distance and time makes peer learning exceedingly difficult. At the same time, when you do manage to get people together, attention spans are even more depressed because of external distractions and the realities of being forced to interact with nothing but a screen for hours on end. In those circumstances, individual or group meetings become particularly important.

All of these considerations are still in play when designing assessments. Is there an advantage in creating multi-part assessments that are connected in time but do not have to all take place synchronously? Is sequence more important than pace? These are all questions that are distorted by the disruptions in the space-time continuum put into place by the nature of digital assessment.

Some questions to consider as you digitally assess your class:

1) What parts of your course benefit more from persistence (asynchronicity) than immediacy (synchronicity)?
2) What parts of your course require immediacy (synchronicity)?
3) How can you take advantage of the characteristics of digital time in your assessment strategies?

Optimizing Instruction for Hybrid Learning

Transitioning to remote teaching in 2020 was, to put it mildly, a chaotic and uneven process. Those of us who looked deeply into what we were doing in the classroom quickly recognized the shortcomings of teaching the same way via video conferencing. Of course, teaching is but a means to an end. The real question is how you preserved learning under those circumstances.

The Hybrid Plus modality described in Chapter 9 requires a deep re-evaluation of how we teach and learn and a recognition that adapting those practices to the shifting strictures of technology is essential to maintaining engagement and success in a particularly fragmented learning environment.

As I redesigned my courses for Covid Summer and beyond, I applied design principles to the new sets of constraints and opportunities that emerged from the process. One way I approached this was to break down my teaching into three elements that applied to virtually all classes: asynchronous elements, synchronous elements, and assessment strategies (which may be done both synchronously and asynchronously). Deconstructing classes into these three categories helps us understand how the different pieces will respond to the limitations of remote teaching best and which areas of student engagement are challenged the most by the shift in modalities.

Digital time and space require us to become mindful of all of the different ways we communicate with our students, how we expect them to communicate with us, and how we expect (hope) they communicate with each other. All of these modalities can further be divided into synchronous and asynchronous interactions. Assessments straddle both of these categories but are important enough to the overall learning process that they demand their own discussion.

Asynchronous Elements

Which parts of instruction are best delivered asynchronously? Most content distribution would fall under this category. While teaching Socratically is not possible asynchronously, its loss is partially compensated for through persistence and replay-ability of online content. Pre-recorded videos are a good substitute for the scaffolding our lectures provide. They should be short so that the content is related in chewable bits (under 10 minutes is ideal). Obviously, written material can be used to supplement this. However, I encourage teachers to remember that the web of 2020 is a profoundly visual medium and this offers many kinds of opportunities to mix and match different forms of communication. Longer bits of faculty-generated content should be broken up and supplemented with visual media wherever possible. Finally, it's important that content in a disconnected medium such as remote learning make narrative sense. It's particularly important to recognize the narrative journey your students are on and to pay particular attention to highlighting the relevance of any particular piece of content or content module to the overall story.

Synchronous Instruction

Synchronous interaction in a world of social distancing is a precious commodity. Therefore, it is essential to think carefully about maximizing the impact of synchronous interactions both between teacher and student(s) as well as among the students. The disinterest and distraction we observe in a physical environment is amplified in remote contexts. Instructor-led class meetings should be centered on an active project and should be designed for small (12 or less) groups of students. I schedule periodic working sessions with the design groups in my class. Class meetings generally consist of instructor-led synchronous group activities focused on clarifying and analyzing content brought to the session by the students as well as the analysis of their own work. In synchronous online sessions lasting 80 minutes, I divide the class into two groups based on mutual interests and meet with each group for 40 minutes sequentially. These sessions are focused on the students working directly on tasks related to the completion of their challenge projects with my guidance and assistance. In these sessions the groups will be working with my assistance on specific activities directly tied to the completion of their projects.

Maximizing opportunities for individualized instruction should be prioritized in all synchronous class planning. There are logistical challenges in meeting with large numbers of students individually but mechanisms to target those struggling the most should be developed within the class structure. I partner with a librarian who is embedded in my class to complement my engagement efforts. She has her own page and can interact with my students independently from me (see also Chapter 4). In effect, she acts as a second teacher and extends my ability to reach out to individual students who may be struggling. Creating opportunities for individual interactions leverages the affordances of instructional methods that are divorced from the strictures of space and time. The most effective synchronous elements of my remote learning class were actually the one-on-one meetings where I checked in with my students, reviewed their work, and, most importantly, answered specific questions that they might have hesitated to ask in front of a larger group.

The most desirable (and hardest to achieve) synchronous interactions are student-initiated interactions. The existence of these indicates that the students are self-motivated to engage with the material socially. The problem is many of our online systems are not optimized for this kind of interaction. As described in the previous chapter, it is essential to encourage students to congregate on their own. Many institutions do not have student-driven videoconferencing platforms or a chat platform within the LMS. Although less-than-ideal, the only real alternative in those circumstances is to direct students to external tools such as Zoom, Slack, and Facetime/iMessage to give them the informal learning tools they will need. Teachers should advocate with their institutions to provide these kinds of informal learning channels to their students.

Assessment Strategies

Traditional assessments administered online are subject to compromise. Simply transferring in-person exams to an online environment invites gaming the exams (cheating). This is an unwinnable war. If, for no other reason than the integrity of the class (and there are many others), reassessing your assessment strategy is a central part of this exercise. The online environment favors authentic assessments. If you think deeply about most in-person assessments, a large part of what they demonstrate is the student's ability to take the test. The student's mastery of the subject is often only a tertiary effect. Why do we test this way? In short, it's what was possible using the technology of pen and paper, which has characterized education in one way or another since Homer. Industrial education merely scaled this with the unintended consequence of dehumanizing the process (see also Chapter 3). New media opens up new possibilities in this area. Students can create meaningful artifacts to demonstrate their learning in a class that have a life far beyond the professor's filing cabinet. Authentic assessment is more meaningful to students and therefore the incentive to cheat is lowered and, furthermore, their ability to cheat is compromised when they are creating something new. Finally, a properly structured act of creation is also an act of teaching. The best way to learn is to teach.

Poor assessment strategies are amplified online as courses quickly turn into box-checking exercises with periodic assessments merely providing the more annoying box. Judgement from a distant instructor is also profoundly depersonalizing and disempowering, both of which are severely destructive to the learning process. Authentic, personalized assessment should therefore be central to any learning process. There are many ways this can be achieved. Students can record video submissions to assignments, create public blogs, or execute semester-long projects such as the Final Portfolio project in my class. Digital technologies give them new ways of expressing their understanding. Effective assessment strategies will leverage these possibilities.

Time and Content are Fluid Concepts in a Digital World

The possibilities created by the affordances of digital communications have made time much more fluid. There are many opportunities created by these time shifts to expand the reach and effectiveness of teaching strategies. The only real timeframe that matters is now the semester. You are no longer constrained by the vagaries of class schedules and physical location in order to teach. We will discuss some of the systemic possibilities of this in our next chapter but for now this new reality should be considered an opportunity to make the class flow according to the needs of the student rather than the schedule. Using the different communication modalities identified above, we can create a table to work through how different tools we use are useful to a greater or lesser degree.

We can break down our class activities based on the kinds of conversations we're having with our students and how we structure conversations among the students. The second chart illustrates how we can create a table using these different communications modalities to analyze how we can use various tools to facilitate different kinds of conversations in our students' learning processes.

Synchronous	Asynchronous
One to Many	One to Many
Many to One	Many to One
Many to Many	Many to Many
One to One	One to One

Time Key->	Synchronous		Asynchronous	
Tools: How would you use?	*One to Many*	*Many to One*	*Many to Many*	*One to One*
Conference Chat	*Pose a question to start a live session*	*Live student feedback to presentation*	*Q & A*	
Discussion Board				
Conference				
Video clip	*Create mini-lectures*	*Student assessment*	*Student presentation*	
Email				
Announce-ments	*Class Updates*			
Documents				
Assess-ments				
Public Writing				
Public Creation				
Canvas Chat				
Interactive Concept Mapping				
Digital Whiteboard				
[Your Tool Here]				
[Your Tool Here]				

In my class, content now forms the scaffolding for the skills that I am trying to teach. This is because content absorption is not usually time dependent. It can be adapted to the needs of exercising skills instead of being compressed by artificial clocks. This approach is flipped from my older teaching strategy. Before, I would teach the skills so students would be able to effectively process the content. Now, I give them a set of tools with which to process any content they might come across, even if it has nothing to do with the study of government. This way, they are actually using the content rather than simply absorbing it, to be excreted only on test day. My class goals are, therefore, centered on what I want them to be able to do rather than what they know. This process also creates opportunities for creating tangible products using the content, as discussed in Chapter 3, as opposed to random occurrences such as test questions which go no further than my filing cabinet.

Pushing content to one side and focusing on skills allows me to focus precious synchronous time, whether in a classroom or via videoconferencing, squarely on fostering the kinds of interactive activities that are so important to the Collaborative Learning approach. As we discussed in Chapter 4, separation of distance and time makes peer learning exceedingly difficult. At the same time, when you do manage to get people together, attention spans are even more compressed because of external distractions and the realities of being forced to stare at a screen for hours on end. The solution is to use technology to optimize your content around the ability of your students to process it. For different students this may vary considerably; if the content is asynchronous that won't matter. In this way, putting content online is *better* than presenting it in the limited spatial and temporal environment we call a classroom.

Fundamentally, teaching in a Hybrid Plus world, where tools are selected and optimized around the needs of learners not technological or administrative convenience (see Chapter 9), requires opening minds to the opportunities that the technology offers. Students and teachers alike will have to spend some time rediscovering what it means to learn. Not all things will be better in this environment, although I am confident that, over time, we will settle on a new normal that optimizes the best of both online and physical environments. Our sacrifices today may help chart a way into a new post-pandemic educational landscape that will be better than the pre-pandemic one. The world will never be the same. It is our responsibility to make sure that this change is for the better. The first step is centering instruction firmly on the learner and then building out from there.

This chart demonstrates how I deconstructed the mechanisms of my own Texas and US Government classes. My courses operate as semester-long challenges. Students select topical challenges that interest them (such as healthcare, the environment, education, social justice, etc.), assess them, and develop strategies for getting US, Texas, or Local government and political systems to address them. The Final Portfolio consists of presenting the final challenge (scope and significance), goals/benchmarks for addressing it, and strategies for achieving them in three different areas of government/politics.

Activity	Pedagogical Purpose	Skills Addressed	Time Mode	Communications Mode	Assessment Strategy	Tools Used (Examples)
Sources	Research for blogs and final portfolio	Digital Literacy, research skills	Asynchronous	Many (*Students*) to Many (*Students*)	Formative	Student links posted to LMS discussion tool, browser, Canvas
Argument Clinic	How to associate arguments with backing sources, how to analyze	Argumentation, analysis, literacy (reading skills)	Synchronous	Many (*Students*) to Many (*Students*)	None	Toulmin Argumentation Model (bit.ly/3nsfwEa), Mindnode (*Concept Mapping Tool*), Zoom (*Videoconferencing Tool*) or in-person
Concept Map	Connecting concepts and creating arguments	Concept creation, analysis	Both	Many (*Students*) to Many (*Students*)	None	**Synchronous**: Mindnode (*Concept Mapping Tool*) and Zoom (*Videoconferencing Tool*) or in-person; **Asynchronous**: Draw.io (*Concept Mapping Tool*) and Google Drive (*Storage and Sharing Tool*)
Content Module	Foundational content	Reading skills, research skills	Asynchronous	One (*Instructor*) to Many (*Students*)	None	Zoom (*Recording Tool for video segments*); OER editable textbook (*for textbook segments*); Canvas (*LMS for Storage and Sharing*)

Activity	Pedagogical Purpose	Skills Addressed	Time Mode	Communications Mode	Assessment Strategy	Tools Used (Examples)
Quiz	Content review	Reading skills	Asynchronous	One (*Instructor*) to One (*Students*)	Gateway	Canvas Quiz tool (*LMS Gateway/Review Assessment*)
Blog	Remixing and presenting content, starts process of Final Portfolio	Writing, analysis, argumentation, presentation	Asynchronous	One (*Student*) to Many (*Students*)	Formative	Student-created Canvas Discussion tool (*Public Writing*)
Comment	Reflection, feedback	Critique, research, feedback	Asynchronous	Many (*Students*) to One (*Student*)	Formative	RISE Model (risemodel.com), Canvas Discussion tool (*LMS Commenting Tool*)
Web Draft	Transfer information from blogs to web site; start building Final Portfolio	Text-to-Image conversion, visual presentation, visual storytelling	Asynchronous	One (*Student*) to Many (*Public, Students*)	Formative	Wordpress, Wix, Weebly, Google Sites, etc. (*Student-Selected Free Web Platform*)
Announce-ments	Course logistics, reminders, meeting invites	Reading Instructions	Both	One (*Instructor*) to Many (*Students*)	None	Announcement Tool in Canvas (*LMS Sharing and Storage*)

Activity	Pedagogical Purpose	Skills Addressed	Time Mode	Communications Mode	Assessment Strategy	Tools Used (Examples)
Individual Meetings	Formative assessment review, student feedback	Critique, learning process reflection	Synchronous	One (Instructor) to One (Student)	Formative	Zoom (Videoconferencing Tool)
Blog Reviews	Formative assessment review, student feedback	Writing, argumentation, critique	Synchronous	One (Instructor) to Many (Students), Many (Students) to-Many (Students)	Formative	Zoom (Videoconferencing Tool) or in-person
Web Draft Reviews	Formative assessment review, student feedback	Visual thinking, argumentation, critique	Synchronous	One (Instructor) to Many (Students), Many (Students) to Many (Students)	Formative	Zoom (Videoconferencing Tool) or in-person
Final Portfolio	Summative, capstone assignment	Visual presentation, information synthesis, content mastery	Asynchronous	One (Student) to Many (Students, Public)	Summative	Wordpress, Wix, Weebly, Google Sites, etc. (Student-Selected Free Web Platform)
Instruction Pages	Instructions, Exemplars	Reading	Asynchronous	One (Instructor) to Many (Students)	None	Zoom (Recording Tool for video segments); Canvas (LMS for Storage and Sharing)

Chapter 6
Digitally Shifting to Create Communities of Learning

Students are not widgets. They have diverse backgrounds and interests and are almost always hard to fit into clean boxes. Individualized instruction, therefore, has to start with the individual. That sounds obvious, but all too often the strictures of time and space get in the way of focusing on the needs of the individual student. Classes come and go according to a bell schedule. Meeting times are not spontaneous; they are held when chaotic schedules allow for them. In this system, students are processed; individualism often gets pushed to the side. It is our job as teachers to press against that.

Most class schedules are organized for organizational convenience, not individual learning needs. As teachers, however, we are often stuck with what we're given due to the size and scheduling of physical spaces. When we don't have to worry about giving up our classroom to the next teacher, losing our students to the next period, or fitting the assigned number of students into a given space, this opens up new possibilities for shuffling our student cohorts. Digital gives us this ability. We need to seize it where we can.

Here are some ideas that don't necessarily require systemic support to institute but, instead, can be done within your own assigned classes or negotiated with other teachers and/or support personnel.

1) Group students according to interest, not schedule and then make the schedule work around their needs.
2) Meet individually with students during class times or outside of class times using a videoconferencing or chat tool.
3) Merge classes in the Learning Management System to increase the number of people in the conversation.
4) As discussed in Chapter 4, bring outside expertise into the class.
5) Share the expertise of your fellow teachers with your classes by bringing them in for "guest lectures" or organizing interdisciplinary activities that combine students from more than one class.

Shifting Time and Space to Create Learner-Centered Instructional Systems

The analog logic of segmenting knowledge and information into course sections is deeply out of sync with new digital realities. One of the themes of *Discovering Digital Humanity* is how a lot of our difficulties are caused by what I call McLuhanesque mistakes, which is translating systems created in response to analog paradigms to digital ones without recognizing the anachronisms as well as opportunities created by that shift in medium.[27] As we go into a far more online educational environment, these anachronisms will proliferate. Many opportunities are created when we shift time and space digitally. We just have to be prepared to grasp them.

Sections are a legacy of the physical world. Classrooms support finite numbers of students. Schedules are driven by the logic of putting students in classrooms at specified regularized times every week. These constraints do not apply to online classes. While there is a legacy from these physical constraints in administrative convenience (and there might be funding implications in some systems), sections have mostly devolved into a measurement detail. In 1999, Donella Meadows analyzed specific areas where we can stimulate systemic change. She developed twelve interconnected "leverage points" that, taken together, push systems in new directions. They were ranked in order of difficulty. Meadows says that measurement variables are the easiest things to change in a given system.[28] Rethinking how we measure units of

---

[27] Haymes, Tom, *Discovering Digital Humanity*, ATBOSH Media, 2021. http://atbosh.com/books/discovering-digital-humanity/
[28] http://donellameadows.org/archives/leverage-points-places-to-intervene-in-a-system/

learning, even on an experimental basis, could result in significant benefits to the overall learning experience of our students.

One of the first things that is likely to come up is the fact that most faculty are paid based on the number of sections that they teach. Rather than exercising the crude expedient of adjusting the number of sections that a faculty member teaches, it would be much more rational to fine tune those adjustments based on students being taught. The limitations placed upon how I teach have far more to do with the size of my sections, which I have little control over, than the number of sections I choose to teach. My pedagogical strategies have to adapt based on whether I have 15 students or 32. I get paid the same amount for either number. The students pay the same amount no matter which section they are in but it's no question that the level of attention I'm able to give each student in the smaller class is much higher than in the larger one.

Some studies have also shown that, particularly if you intend on teaching in any style other than strict instructionism (objectivism) (see Chapter 2), smaller class sizes may be necessary. In a 2019 review article, Susan Taft, Karen Kesten, and Majeda M. el-Banna mapped out the optimal class sizes for online learning based on pedagogical approach. They concluded that, "pedagogical requisites should drive the choice of online class sizes."[29] Applying "constructivist" methods for teaching are

---

[29] Taft, S.H., Kesten, K., & El-Banna, M.M. (2019). One size does not fit all: Toward an evidence- based framework for determining online course enrollment sizes in higher education. *Online Learning, 23*(3), 188-233. doi:10.24059/olj.v23i3.1534 at https://files.eric.ed.gov/fulltext/EJ1228823.pdf p. 222

significantly constrained in online classes numbering more than 23 students.[30]

There is little to no reason to group students in this manner in an online environment. The space-time limitations that created the logic of sections simply don't exist there. Instead of creating space and time-centered divisions, we need to think about building learner-centered networks. What would student-centered "sections" look like? I argue in Chapter 9 that online classes could be identified as either totally asynchronous or requiring some level of synchronous interaction to give students a better idea of the expectations of interaction a given class would have. As a starting point, this would be a better way of identifying how the class would work to the student than a random section number and would furthermore set student expectations accordingly when they signed up for a particular course of instruction.

Personalizing instruction is also facilitated by a section-less system of learning. I try to tailor my instruction around the interests of a given student since that will provide a more meaningful instructional experience for him or her. Having a larger pool of students to choose from (through consolidating all of my sections) makes this far easier when it comes to group formation. Creating different ways to mix-and-match students while maintaining the ability to create working groups of learners would allow us to design more individualized pathways for learning.

This is not just a convenience factor. Creating systems based on student communities rather than sections would allow for a far more nuanced approach to

---

[30] Ibid, p. 223

creating learning centered on communities of practice and opens the doors to explorations of interdisciplinary approaches to learning. As Linda DeAngelo pointed out in a 2014 study, retention is greatly enhanced by students developing networks outside the traditional classroom.[31] Sections divide learners arbitrarily. We need to be looking for network opportunities to connect them instead of splitting them for administrative convenience.

Sections also tend to wall off disciplines from one another. Allowing students to subscribe to a cohort of interdisciplinary instructors working together can reap huge benefits. For instance, I teach my government class as a design studio. Coordinating with English Composition, Design, and, perhaps, Student Success faculty, we could develop an integrated approach to a student's (or preferably a learning community of students') learning experience(s). Interdisciplinary approaches have been shown to lead to better outcomes.

Finally, as I will suggest again in Chapter 9, focusing on smaller and shorter segments of learning, which getting rid of traditional sections would facilitate, makes our systems of learning much more antifragile. Small, focused learning communities are going to be much nimbler in the chaotic teaching/scheduling environments for the near- to medium-term future.

There are, no doubt, significant systemic hurdles around getting rid of the administrative convenience that sections offer. The current crisis, however, will not be sympathetic to those institutions that hold tightly to outdated shibboleths. Using sections as a tool for dividing

---

[31] De Angelo, Linda, "Programs and Practices that Retain Students from the First to Second Year," *New Directions for Institutional Research* #160, pp. 53-75

up students and faculty largely for administrative convenience should be looked at carefully. There seems to be little logic pertaining to learning and retention that supports their continued existence. If anything, the opposite is true. In a digital world there is little administrative logic to continuing to use them either.

This logic extends beyond our current circumstances, however. With an online-focused hybrid schedule, physical environments will need to be scheduled on an ad hoc basis anyway so, even when we return to a "new normal," sections can still start to be retired as a metric. Online communities of practice can be used to drive student sorting even in a hybrid model. The exigencies of the pandemic are severely testing our institutions of higher learning. We can either collapse under the strain or use this tragedy as an opportunity to make learning better for our students. Developing strategies for phasing out traditional sections would allow us to focus on using quality to overcome adversity.

Rethinking Tools for Hybrid and Online Learning

Getting rid of sections is enabled by a shift in how we teach our classes. Over the last two decades, higher education has increased its reliance on online learning as a mechanism for increasing its reach, growing enrollment, and containing costs. For some students, this has been a godsend. It enables many to attend college amid competing pressures from work and family. However, colleges continue to struggle with issues of quality and connecting to isolated learners taking online courses.

Hybrid instruction leverages the strengths of online and in-person instruction, but figuring out the right balance between synchronous and asynchronous learning remains a thorny challenge. Online learning does not benefit all students equally. In a study published in 2019, Spiros Protopsaltis and Sandy Baum observed that:

> Creating access to programs is a step forward, but only if those programs succeed in providing meaningful educational opportunities to students with minimal levels of academic preparation who need to develop their self-discipline, time management, and learning skills—not just have access to a specific body of information. As we seek to improve the quality of online education and reverse its poor record in an effort to ensure that it not only serves more students, but also serves them well, it is critical to promote regular and substantive student-instructor interaction.[32]

The lack of student-instructor interaction should not surprise us. My colleague Bryan Alexander once observed in a talk at the New Media Consortium that technology is adopted by humans in two phases. In the first phase, we view new technology as a more efficient but analogous version of existing technology. Hence the automobile was a "horseless carriage" first. In the second phase, the technology reshapes our fundamental processes. Online learning is still in what Alexander refers to as a first-level technological paradigm. We are largely adapting "traditional" classes, not restructuring instruction. Our

---

[32] Spiros Protopsaltis and Sandy Baum, "Does Online Education Live Up to Its Promise? A Look at the Evidence and Implications for Federal Policy," at http://mason.gmu.edu/~sprotops/OnlineEd.pdf, p. 2

mental model starts with, "How do I teach my 'regular' class online?" This kind of question implies that we are still in the "horseless carriage" mode of understanding how technology will change instruction.

The result is a very uneven learning environment in the online sphere. Some functions, such as content distribution, are well-provided for, while others, such as tools for sharing, are not as effectively supported, leading to a bias toward what Papert and Harel referred to as the Intructionist mode of teaching over more Constructionist approaches.[33] Those populations who have been well trained in the consumption of content and its regurgitation do well. Those with poor learning skills or those who seek deeper understanding of the topic are often left frustrated, isolated and disconnected.

This also raises deep qualitative versus quantitative questions. If we are content to measure success with grades over achievement, the results look good. If, however, we wish to achieve lasting, deeper learning, we must examine what is going on in both physical and virtual spaces and develop appropriate tools to meet the challenges of achieving authentic teaching and learning.

---

[33] Papert, Seymour and Idit Harel, *Constructionism*, Ablex Publishing, 1991

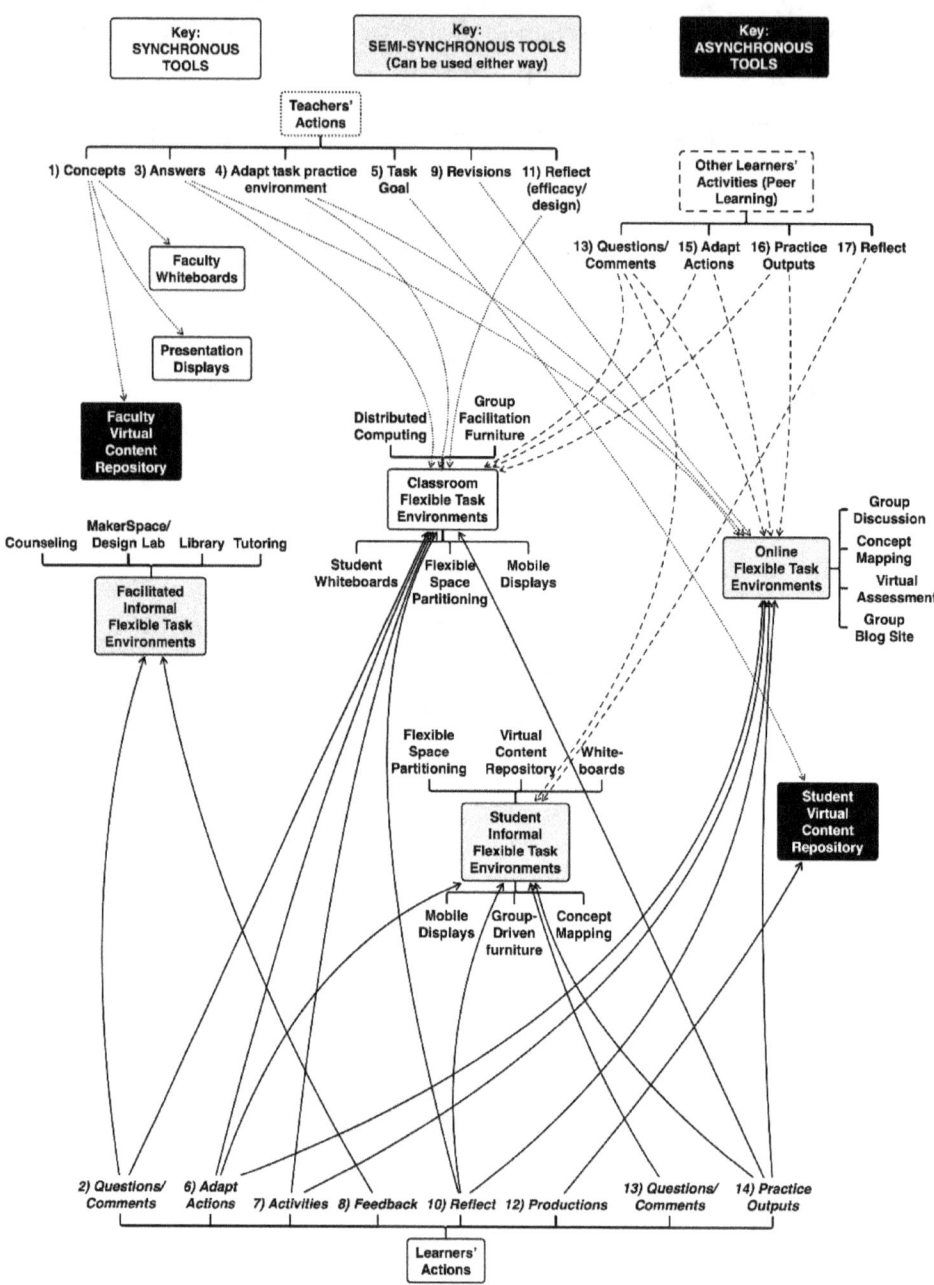

Using an approach based on Laurillard's **Conversational Frameworks**, I find that the one thing that immediately jumps out is that learning requires a broad set of tools to be effective. One common theme in-person and online, however, is a need for flexible task environments that augment learning conversations. Properly designed hybrid instruction (partially online and partially in-person) gives both teacher and learner access to the widest range of complementary tools. Online instruction offers persistence and repetition difficult to achieve within the temporal and physical constraints of a traditional classroom. Physical environments, and the people who inhabit them, provide a level of human interaction and immediacy of response difficult to replicate virtually. Effective hybrid instruction should combine the best of both (for more on tools, see Chapter 1).

However, hybrid classes suffer from the same technological blinders as fully online classes ("How do I teach half my 'regular' class online?"). When hybrid works, it can be very effective, but I believe the relative scarcity of hybrid classes is because doing them effectively requires a total deconstruction of the activities in a class, followed by an adaptation of them to the appropriate modalities of physical and online paradigms. This is challenging and forces the teacher to closely examine the modalities of his or her instruction. Mapping instruction onto Laurillard's framework may provide an easier pathway to deconstructing instruction.

This is only half the challenge. Deep analysis of how courses are being taught in the online/hybrid environment will quickly lead to the conclusion that physical environments will also have to adapt to better meet the needs of asynchronous students. One strategy is to view hybrid classes as online classes with physical support, instead of vice versa. This will help both faculty and institutions develop second-order technological approaches, because it forces them to work backwards to the physical paradigm. Some for-profit institutions such as Strayer and the University of Phoenix that are heavily dependent on online instruction are already doing this and starting to build specially designed physical spaces to support their online students.[34]

A systematic, learner-centric approach leads us to logical conclusions about how both online and physical learning environments should adapt to support hybrid instruction. For instance, spaces where faculty can meet with varying groups of hybrid students at irregular intervals should be part of the physical design and management of campuses supporting hybrid students.

Furthermore, augmenting informal support for teaching and learning, such as tutoring, counseling, making, and library services, will better support students who benefit from the asynchronous nature of online learning but struggle with learning outcomes absent the physical mentorship of college personnel (see Chapter 4).

Meeting the needs of all students requires the proper application of technology and also an understanding of human nature. It is easy to imagine a landscape where all courses are "hybrid," but plotting a

---

[34] Lindsey McKenzie, "Changing Spaces," *Inside Higher Education*, August 14, 2019 at https://www.insidehighered.com/digital-learning/article/2019/08/14/changing-role-physical-campuses-online-education

course to get there will remain a challenge. We must engage in an ongoing conversation about how technology reshapes instruction. The central theme of this book is that learning is a difficult process and the mental, physical, and virtual tools available to both the teacher and learner must be aligned around augmenting human learning, not administrative convenience. Digital technology gives us the ability to achieve that. It is our responsibility as teachers to implement strategies that support online learning synchronously and collaboratively wherever possible and to advocate for systemic changes such as better software (Chapter 7) or physical environments (Chapter 4) that support learning whenever or wherever it might occur.

PART III

Mapping New Realities for the Digital Age

- *Mindfully Create Learning Experiences*
- *Chart Learning Journeys*
- *Navigate Uncertainty with a Steady Compass Fixed on Community*

Chapter 7

Creating Learner-Centered Virtual Environments

SPACE — Don't Settle for Tools That Undermine Your Teaching Strategies

STRATEGY 7

Our students think of learning not as a series of disconnected events but, rather, as a coherent whole. They have been trained from an early age to accept that this is "what school is like" and to accept the circumstances they are placed into as a necessary stepping-stone to an ephemeral future. Statements like "school isn't for me" or "I don't understand learning" should be viewed as an indictment of the system we have placed that student in, not the student. These are the products of a system where conformity is valued more than individuality. Our tools often reflect this attitude. We accept them for what they are rather than demanding they do what we need them to do.

The reality is that everyone is constantly learning but often it is lessons that we don't intend to teach about parts of the experience we often dismiss as trivial. Having an uncomfortable classroom chair is an inconvenience for a short period of time, but if it becomes part of a daily grind lasting hours at a time, it starts to overwhelm the other experiences that might happen in that space. Likewise, if you spend most of your time fighting with the Learning Management System (LMS) while trying to communicate and express yourself, the experience will be one of fighting with the LMS, not those activities that expand your learning.

Students also make assumptions about the tools available to them; it's part of your responsibility to both make tools accessible and available to them. This semester, which has begun (and will likely finish) remotely, I had a student complain that she couldn't make a particular videoconferencing tool work technically. I pointed out to her that I was using a different platform with far lower barriers to entry. She was in the next session with no problems. Technological inconveniences, such as bad seating, can quickly escalate to an absolute barrier as much as the technical challenges of connecting to a poorly-designed videoconferencing platform. All too often, learning is subsumed, or prevented altogether, by the noise of the environment in which it is supposed to take place. Environments can also greatly facilitate our learning conversations.

We have a responsibility as teachers to be a part of shaping our learning environments. We have more control over them than ever before. Often, however, the choices of the tools that shape those environments have been made by people who have never been inside a classroom and, as such, don't have a clear understanding of the complexities of the interactions between teachers and students. If you have a classroom where the desks are bolted to the floor, your options are severely constrained. However, there are very few circumstances in our software tools where that is necessarily the case. It is often a simple matter to move to a different digital "classroom" altogether. Yet, we often treat those digital tools as being every bit as bolted down as furniture can be.

In a classroom, you have to work around the shortcomings of furniture, display technology, and lighting, to cite just a few examples. In the digital world, it's far easier to adapt our environments to the needs of teaching and learning. If a videoconferencing platform fails to meet the needs of your students, either because it is inaccessible or because its tools are designed for a business environment, not an educational one, it's trivial to switch to a different platform. There is no reason why we should accept the kinds of limitations in our digital environments that we do in our physical environments and yet we do.

Of course, it's best to adopt tools from the outset that prioritize teaching, learning, and community over other considerations, such as administrative convenience. When I first started teaching with technology, the possibilities were limited by the realities of technical considerations. This is almost never the case anymore. Most technical limitations have been driven to the fringes. We can now get into cars and drive 200 or even 2,000 miles with little fear that they will fail us along the way. This was not the case a century ago. Digital technology has evolved at a much faster rate than the realities of engineering reliable cars (and the crashes are usually far less consequential). We have at our disposal an array of reliable technologies which can help us communicate with our students; even when we do encounter the occasional glitch, there are almost always alternative systems.

As we discussed in Chapter 2, learning is fundamentally a series of conversations. The biggest change that the internet has brought into our lives has been to provide us with a plethora of communication tools. It is our responsibility to use them to give our students voices. We can use them to create digital environments where the student is empowered to create and learn. We need to reflect on how these new realities impact our roles as teachers and guides through the confusing maze that confronts most students as they embark on learning journeys. Technology can be used to make those paths clearer or it can be used to make them more confusing and intimidating. The choices and demands we make as we select software impacts which of those two realities our students are thrust into.

1) Understand that you are creating a digital ecosystem for your students.
2) Think through your tasks before linking them with tools (see Chapters 1 and 4 for more on how to do that). If the linkage doesn't work, adapt the tools before compromising the task.
3) Put yourself in the shoes of your students as you approach software. Learner-centric teaching and learning should not be compromised because of limitations in digital tools.
4) Become an active participant in the selection of digital tools and don't compromise your learning tasks; change the tool.

Opening Doors Instead of Windows

While I generally avoid direct comparisons between the classroom and the learning management system, they do share one thing in common: they are both constructed environments that both student and teacher have to live in. In the classroom, there are real limitations in terms of physical space and purchased equipment and furniture. Those kinds of limitations don't exist in our virtual environments. As I argued in Chapter 1, our tools should augment our purposes. The purpose of learning is to form connections. Tools designed for that purpose should therefore connect rather than separate. The legacy of app-based software environments, however, separates tasks (and people) instead of connecting them. This design philosophy used to be required due to technological limitations, but there is no longer any reason for it and this artificially stunts what we think we can do as teachers.

Before computers, anything could be an assignment or project. The limits imposed were primarily those of the logistics of space and assessment. As we gradually imposed technology, in many cases for efficiency's sake, the limits of creativity were increasingly bounded. As class sizes and teacher responsibilities expanded from dozens to hundreds, normative technology became increasingly necessary, if for no other reason than crowd control. If you have nothing but individual tutorials, you can adapt assignments to the needs of the individual student, and technology imposes few constraints. If you are dealing with 100 students with a constrained amount of time and resources, efficiencies become necessary and all students are required to be treated the same. This means that tests and assignments have to be standardized, if for no other reason than being able to grade them in a reasonable amount of time. Communication strategies get normalized into lectures to support those assignments. Technologies such as blackboards, whiteboards, audio amplification, overhead projectors, and film projectors evolved to support those needs.

We added to these constraints, starting in the 1970s and 80s, the realities of early computing that operated under severe technical limitations. This tended to lead to less-complex task-specific applications. This shift further constrained assignments due to the technical limitations of students and faculty. You didn't draw in a word processor. You typed in it, because technically that was all it was able to do given the limitations in RAM, display, and printing technology. Economics took over in the 80s; companies took this proprietary notion of software and created vast fortunes selling increasingly specialized widgets for increasingly specialized tasks. Advances in processing power often led to more specialization rather than creating rich ecosystems of connectivity.

I have always been frustrated with applications. I am far more interested in expressing and connecting ideas then I am in messing with an application. To put it another way, I have always been more interested in the music than the piano. This is how I operate as a content creator; this is how I operate as a teacher; and this is how I want my students to be able to operate. As Alan Kay once put it, "for most people, the piano has been the biggest thing to turn people away from music for the rest of their lives."[35] Music driven by traditional instruments is hard. I was naturally drawn to it as a child, but I never learned the patience necessary to master the tool, so I gave up in frustration. But

---

[35] https://www.youtube.com/watch?v=bC7x_qntM0g at 0:52

I have maintained a lifelong fascination with the idea of music, and its intricate patterns. If I had had access to some of the music-making tools that exist today, my life might have taken a different path.

The tools of what we call "technology" have often become equally hard and complex as we have connected applications instead of people. As Jaron Lanier, who worked with Kay at Atari, said in a 2018 book, "The way we've designed the tools requires that people comply totally with an infinite number of arbitrary actions. We really have turned humanity into lab rats that are trained to run mazes. I really think on just the most fundamental level we are approaching digital technology in the wrong way."[36] Learning is a complex enough maze without layering over it a series of technological mazes. All too often, we prioritize the paintbrush over the painting.

As a teacher, I'm struggling to get my students to learn to paint their own visions of the world. It is often a monumental struggle retraining those who have learned from school that the highest art is understanding the vision of others. Add to that a suite of complex tools designed with the philosophy of received rather than constructed knowledge and you've created an unnecessarily unforgiving learning environment. "Learning" Management Systems are one of the last bastions of single-purpose tools. An assessment is an assessment. Period. You may have three or four different flavors of assessment but once you leave those behind, it isn't an assessment anymore and, more importantly, only assessments go in the grade book. Finally, the application starts from the premise that the most important aspect of assessments is

---

[36] Fisher, Adam. *Valley of Genius*. Grand Central Publishing. Kindle Edition

security. Therefore, the default definition of collaboration is cheating. These design decisions are not made by the teacher or the student but, rather, through the design of the software.

This design philosophy goes against the vision of education as a holistic experience; one that changes the learner. Shouldn't a student be able to designate any piece of content as a submission to an assignment and allow the teacher to grade it? Shouldn't the tools conform to the needs of the student first, the teacher second, and the logic of the software a distant third? Learning is a process of communication. Humans communicate in a vast array of ways, from music to painting to writing to speaking. Effective learning must meet the students where they are; anything that gets in the way of that must be minimized or removed. Software must facilitate a broad panoply of communication channels, not stifle them. It's high time we rethought what that means. That path lies through a door not chosen a quarter century ago.

Designing a class in a Learning Management System (LMS) is like programming. The teacher or designer is programming the pathways that a student should take as he or she works through the mechanics of the class. However, the first pathway that has to be programmed is the actual content and skills that the student is expected to travel through over the course of the term or class. This pathway should take priority over any other narrative pathway. As I discuss in the next chapter, in any given class there is a narrative that must be clear. This narrative has to work for both the teacher and student, and both have to be carefully programmed. The teacher should have a wide array of storytelling tools just like in the physical classroom. All too often, however, the software throws up barriers and walls at odds with the programming goal of either narrative. These barriers are a consequence of decisions taken in the 1980s and 90s that charted the path of how software works. Instead of creating relationships and connections between people and ideas, the focus became one of creating relationships between software applications. This framework can still be seen in our software environments today, even *within* applications such as an LMS.

As we explored in Chapter 1, tools need to be built up from tasks, not the other way around. The tasks of learning should be clearly defined so that clear pedagogical pathways can be established. Only after that has occurred should the tools necessary to achieve those goals be designed, preferably, as much as possible, by the users themselves. As I try to teach people to teach and learn with technology, I am constantly fighting against the magic and mystery component of computing. Much of that comes from overly complex solutions to necessary tasks. LMSes are particularly susceptible to this kind of mission creep; the result is a confusing maze of applications, within the system, that tend to distract and separate students and teachers from their fundamental task: connecting ideas through teaching and learning.

However, if the tools in our box are broken, adapting them to useful purposes becomes more difficult. Software should be among the most easily adaptable of these tools, but often it is not. This is largely due to the mindset with which most people approach software. It is treated as a fixed object, like a table or a chair. You make an investment in it and you're stuck with it. Years ago, a former chancellor at my institution was quoted, after being shown an unworkable software package, "We paid for it.

We better use it." Never mind the implications it had on all of the people and processes it impacted. This kind of thinking is antithetical to task-driven technology usage. Software should be our most flexible tool. Yet, often, its limitations are what drive instruction. Indeed, entire courses are built around learning how to adapt humans to specific kinds of technology. This extends the insanity beyond the walls of institutions as we train "word processing specialists" whose job it is to operate a tool rather than understand the task the tool was designed for or to adapt or discard that particular tool when it is no longer relevant to the task.

As we design our classes, learning should always be the priority. Tools need to support the design of our classes, not get in the way of them. Teaching is hard. Learning is hard. The last thing we need is for the tools to get in the way of what we're trying to accomplish. Learner-centric teaching has always required an antifragile approach to design, because the unique demands of the individual learner will challenge any system, no matter how carefully designed. As Douglas Adams wrote, "A common mistake that people make when trying to design something completely foolproof is to underestimate the ingenuity of complete fools."[37] Humans tend to bend practically every technology they are confronted with. Our software platforms need to be a little more like a guitar and a little less like china. Brittle systems will break, not bend, in the face of adversity. You don't need a pandemic to do that. You just need human beings dealing with life to do that. The pandemic has just shown us the cracks.

---

[37] Adams, Douglas, *Mostly Harmless*, Ballantine Books, 1993, p. 135

This brittleness is a legacy of app-based thinking that creates very specific roles for different sets of class tools. Alan Kay, whom I quoted earlier, was a veteran of Xerox PARC in the 1970s and responsible for many of the conceptual leaps that made early computing possible. He conceived of a device that was very similar in many respects to the iPad – in 1968. The key element of this conceptual "Dynabook," as Kay named it, was that it represented a computing device that supported the needs of the user by being portable and responsive to the user at all times. Think of it as a Swiss-Army knife of computing. He went on to develop many key aspects of the Graphical User Interface (GUI) at Xerox and has subsequently done much work developing the relationship between computing and learning.

Kay thinks that computing took a left turn after his development of the Smalltalk-based Xerox systems. Specifically, Apple, and later Microsoft, took the GUI-based ideas from the Xerox systems but left behind a fundamental design principle: the idea of app-less systems based on tasks, not applications. Some of that resurfaced in the late 80s with Bill Atkinson's HyperCard. HyperCard connected concepts and ideas in infinitely rearrangeable sets of "cards." You could create flexible and easily reprogrammable databases of information in this way. I remember realizing at the time that we had taken a profound step toward the Star Trek computer with this software and, indeed, it very quickly led to the development of the ultimate HyperCard Stack: Tim Berners-Lee's World Wide Web in the early 1990s.

What these approaches all had in common was their emphasis on connecting content over segregating it. Just like ideas, there is no technical reason that content blocks cannot simply describe what they are and then be infinitely relatable to other content blocks based on the connections you need to make. That was the essence of Berner-Lee's approach to web development, but this thread was also not lost at Apple. Building on HyperCard, the ideas of Alan Kay (an Apple Fellow in the 1980s), Jed Harris of Apple's Advanced Technology Group developed OpenDoc in the early 1990s with the idea that software needed to transition back, "from an application-centered paradigm to a content-centered paradigm (automatically invoking whatever components are required to handle the content)."[38] This project fell victim to Apple's financial troubles in the late 90s. More importantly, with it died the strand of technological development that focused on the user's needs first and built applications around tasks. Coincidentally, LMSes started developing around the same time as OpenDoc died. None have ever embraced any of its essential elements.

While the content is often very important, it is the connections between content that are essential to teaching and learning. Content can always be reclaimed, but it is how we use content, especially in a world of Google, that is truly important today. Developing the skills necessary to process, connect, repurpose, and create with content is much more important than the memorization of information that can be retrieved at any time from computer networks.

But we can take this a step further and connect tools as if they were content. Much of my work is focused on

---

[38] Curbow and Dykstra-Erickson, "Designing the OpenDoc Human Interface," ACM, 1997, p. 83

what can broadly be described as linking "content" with different kinds of "content." Any tool is analogous to content in the hands of its wielder because, like sources and other forms of content, its very nature shapes the stories it can create. Connecting tools forms the basis for creating spaces of learning and innovation that in themselves form content. This relationship is like the relationship between words, paragraphs, and this narrative. Tools form sets of tools that form environments. Those environments in turn connect to stories of ideas which are shaped by tools of communication. It's the connections that shape the human outcomes of those stories. Connecting communication and environments to humans is the final and most complex interconnection that has to be made. Being able to constantly adapt and reshape our environments and communication to meet the needs of the humans within them is essential to the cultivation of ideas, whether they are in the form of learning or innovations. Unnecessarily specialized and non-customizable tools retard that final synergy.

While the nature of objects and tools in physical environments create limits to how far you can customize, there are no such limits in digital environments. Yet we insist on building tools that are inflexible and channel communication and functionality down prescribed paths. There are reasons for this. People are uncomfortable in a world without constraints and seek familiar metaphors. People are more comfortable rearranging a room than a piece of software because it is easier to see what you're doing. Metaphors for a chair are not necessary because you can see a chair. Software, however, has to create metaphors out of its code. In an internal memo while at Apple in the

1980s, Alan Kay advocated a similar approach to software: start with the familiar.

> The approach in getting users to tailor sophisticated software is to first get them to edit drawings, spreadsheet calculations, and text as they have done in the past. Then show them how spreadsheet tactics can be used to make custom controllable graphics objects. Finally, when they want to crack the hood, reveal that the word processor is just another data-driven graphics program -- similar to the ones they have been making but with a little more mechanism.[39]

We need a more visual and content neutral LMS. In this quote, Kay suggests a possible pathway forward. First, create a set of familiar building blocks.[40] However, don't restrict how you use them. Second, make those connections visible ("crack the hood") in order to make it easier for both teacher and student to create visual pathways through the course from a technical perspective. More importantly, create those pathways so that they can also be seen from a narrative perspective. Kay proposes a graphical way of representing this in his proposal. He was not the first to present the ideas of visual, object-oriented programming. Ivan Sutherland, one of Kay's mentors, developed a revolutionary application in the 1960s called Sketchpad, which allowed drawing on the screen. Most importantly for Kay, however, "Sketchpad has only one style, that of causing desired relationships between variables to happen." (Alan Kay, 1984, p. 4) Graphics make

---

[39] Alan Kay, 1984, p. 6
[40] I have written for the ShapingEDU Project at Arizona State University about how Legos are a good analogy for redesigning systems of educational tool sets at http://shapingedu.asu.edu/teaching-toolset-triangle-project/Legos

it easier to see *relationships* and *connections*, both of which are also fundamental to the process of teaching and learning. Making an online course out of graphical elements that can be connected and reconnected in this manner would allow us to program in a way that is complementary to how we program our learning pathways, both as students and as teachers. For many years the limitations of processing and storage space limited how we used graphics. In many ways this was a technical challenge that OpenDoc struggled with in the context of 1990s technology. This is no longer the case.

We are now faced with monolithic LMSes that are a product of their design processes. Some of them are quite good at meeting their designed goals. However, those goals are often at odds with real learning because they assume the strictures of industrial processes, such as tests (and their attendant security needs), regimented course plans (often created apart from the teacher-student relationship), and attendance/"activity," which measure learning as "butts in seats" rather than comprehension. So, what is a teacher to do? First of all, recognize that the boundaries of your LMS are no more the boundaries of learning than the walls of your classroom are.

Moreover, as we have discussed in numerous other parts of this book, those walls are ephemeral and timeless in nature. In other words, you can bring ideas into the LMS or send your students out to find them in the vast universe that is the online world today. This also applies to tools that help you connect those ideas. One of my favorite sets of tools are those that facilitate Mindmapping/Concept Mapping, because they can turn ideas into visual constructs that can be manipulated and connected much like object-oriented programming does. I am not aware of any LMS that contains these tools, but there are many examples outside the LMS. Google Drive allows me to use an open-source tool called draw.io to share concept maps among my students. Using these tools facilitates my ability to teach what's important: making connections between ideas. When the box becomes too restrictive, leave it.

I am not sanguine about the logistical issues and constraints that throwing too many unstructured ideas and tools at my students creates. However, as we discuss in the next chapter, it is possible to create roadmaps to navigate students through complex learning journeys. I am hopeful that the last 25 years of regimented app-oriented software may be a blip and that we will revert back to the much more human-centered approach advocated by Kay and others in the 1970s. The barriers to entry (or exit, as you like) are lowering every day as basic interactions with applications become less complex and ubiquitous. I can do on my phone what it took massive computer power to achieve as recently as the 1990s. We must not, however, become overwhelmed by the sheer number of possibilities that exist or that will become a new set of constraints. This is an easier problem to overcome as long as we focus on what we want to do as teachers and learners and rigorously design systems of facilitating applications around our necessary tasks.

As I noted earlier in this chapter, learning is hard. There are no longer any technical excuses to limit ourselves in this way. The tools that we create to facilitate learning should not make it more difficult. It's high time we assume control as teachers and demand better in the service of learning.

Chapter 8

Mapping the Digital Learning Journey

Our students are lost. This was true before COVID-19. I can count on one hand the number of students who have come through my class that have any idea what education is about. We need to be having honest discussions with our students about how education works. It is essential that they construct context to begin to understand how the various pieces of our courses work together. This discussion is also critical to the task of getting them beyond the challenges of Transactional Teaching as described in Chapter 3. However, this does not absolve us from our role as guides through a confusing landscape of learning systems.

Narratives are extremely important in the disconnected environment most students experience in online learning. While there are challenges in keeping a remote class on track, there are also useful tools that can mitigate the fact that you are not seeing your students twice a week in a physical space.

There are a number of areas where online learning is actually a more efficient means of communicating material to students than lecturing in front of a class. If you lecture something, it can be adapted to an asynchronous object. Starting with instructions themselves, but also including required readings (preferably with an electronic textbook that can be sliced and diced to fit within your overall class narrative), and short video presentations where I can curate and scaffold the information and highlight those aspects most likely to help students through the course. As we discussed in Chapter 5, traditional narratives should not constrain our thinking about the story *of* the class. For instance, the targeted use of assessment strategies can be optimized for online learning, but also form a critical part of the class narrative. These strategies should not be perceived as a detour or rest stop along the way. Instead, they should be perceived by the students as a central part of a class narrative that leads toward a tangible end. Assessment is inherently weakened when it is not coupled with a formative strategy. That means that any good story has to stop and look back at the road already taken in order to see the road ahead.

1) Instruction was becoming more disconnected before the pandemic. Provide your students with a clear structure and logic for *everything* they're doing in the class.

2) Act as a guide, not a driver. Create a system where the students guide themselves through the process with your help.
3) Understand the different storytelling tools (visual, written, oral, etc.) at your disposal and how they work differently in different circumstances (synchronous vs. asynchronous; proximate vs. distant, etc.).
4) Maximize your storytelling effectiveness by learning to play your storytelling tools like instruments in an orchestra. It's all about the music, not the instruments.
5) The audience is the author. Never forget that the only story that matters is the one going on in the learner's head.

Designing Digital Narratives

Humans tell each other stories as a way of making sense of the world. One of the profound deficits of social isolation is that it puts barriers to our ability to share stories. Storytelling is a two-way process. The storyteller requires feedback from the listener to know that the story is being heard. Furthermore, we often lose sight of the story that is unfolding across the entirety of our courses. The small stories have to make sense in the overall narrative. In the end the student is the ultimate storyteller because they are forming impressions and ordering the story as they see it, not necessarily as the teacher intended to tell it. If that part of the process fails, it's all for naught. The audience is the author.

Our classes are often by their very nature collages, but they must be carefully constructed to highlight and not obscure the intended pathway to the end. Simplicity of the meta-narrative is crucial here. Everything in my class is oriented toward a single goal: a tangible work product at the end of the semester. *How* my students get there is less of a concern to me than *whether* they get there. However, it is my responsibility as a teacher to show them the way there through my design of the narrative.

The temptations of the digital canvas are to provide a wide range of activities and opportunities for exploration. However, there is a danger here of leading students down alleys and then having the class become about the detour, not the intended thoroughfare. One of my favorite documentaries, *Objectified*, is an exploration of design in the modern world. I once watched it during a flight to a conference where I was scheduled to give a presentation. Braun designer Dieter Rams is featured in the documentary, and his famous dictum, "less, but better," resonated with me at that moment as I considered the story I was about to tell at the conference. I resolved to remove 5 of the 25 slides from my 60-minute presentation. They represented interesting information, but the challenge presented by Rams to me was to ruthlessly examine every element of my narrative and determine what was central to my story and what was not. In the digital world, there is always a temptation to add one more slide because it is easy and free. Taking out slides is a much more difficult task because it is an exercise in design. My subsequent presentation was one of the most favorably received I've ever given.

These same principles must apply to the narratives we construct online (and in person). One of my mentors in grad school, Roy Godson, taught me that in delivering a lecture to an audience, they are unlikely to remember more than three things from a given session, no matter its length. I would take that further and say that the audience will also paste together those three points into a narrative that makes sense to them. A colleague related to me that a student once answered a question on his exam about the difference between State Department employees and Department of Defense employees as, "State Department employees are like cows grazing in a field." When he asked the student what prompted her answer, she replied, "you said they see the world in 'shades of grays.'" All narratives are subject to contextualization.

I face special challenges in my class design because it doesn't follow the typical narrative structure of lecture-review-test-lecture-review-final that most students have come to expect from college courses. Therefore, in addition to the content discussion in my class, I have to explicitly compete with the narrative that exists in 90% of their other classes. One of my chief concerns in moving my class online was that having this conversation would prove to be more difficult. I feared that they would become hopelessly lost because I was leading them down unfamiliar pathways in their approaches to surviving school. I usually have to devote considerable class time to meta-conversations about the nature of the class itself. These kinds of conversations are by their very nature difficult online. This makes creating clean and clear pathways essential to the success of my pedagogical goals, both in-person and online.

Enter design principles. I am ruthless in stripping away extraneous cues in my class narrative. I now have a simple step-by-step diagram set up like a game board metaphor. I have three thoughts for my students: 1) This class is different; 2) Follow the board and do what it says; 3) Everything in this class is focused on creating a Final Portfolio product that will be yours to keep. I have also added to this a layer of iconography that provides a visual clue to the student about the *kind* of task they are performing at any given time.

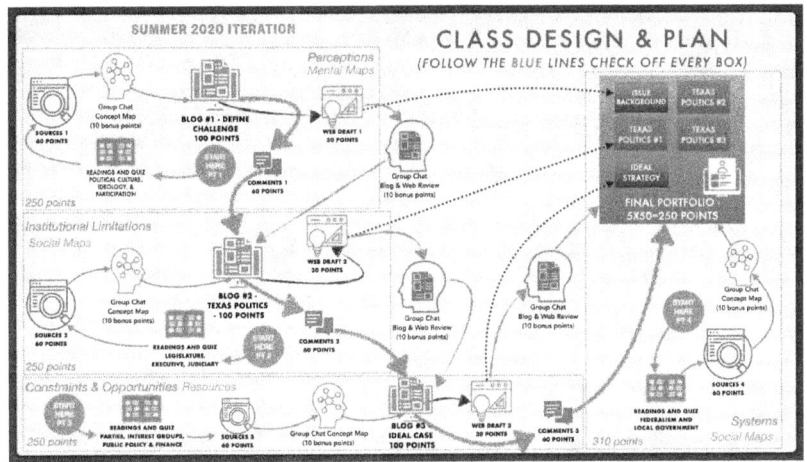

*Class Design Overview for my Class.
The Thick Line is the Narrative Path*

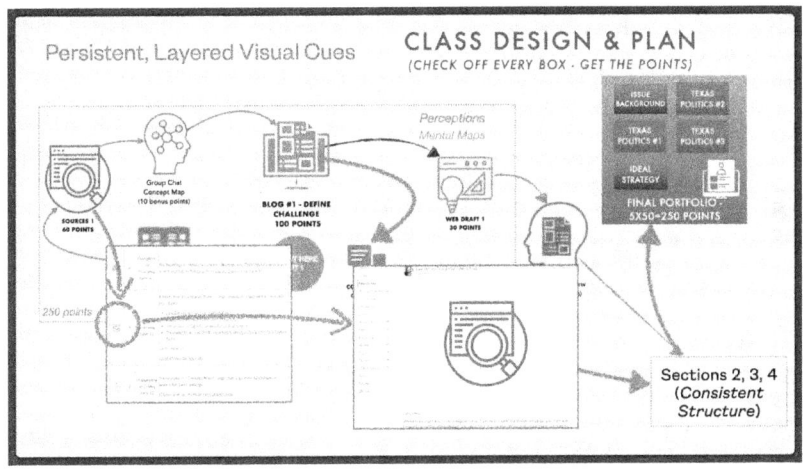

*The Use of Iconography Linking Activities
to Narrative Pathways*

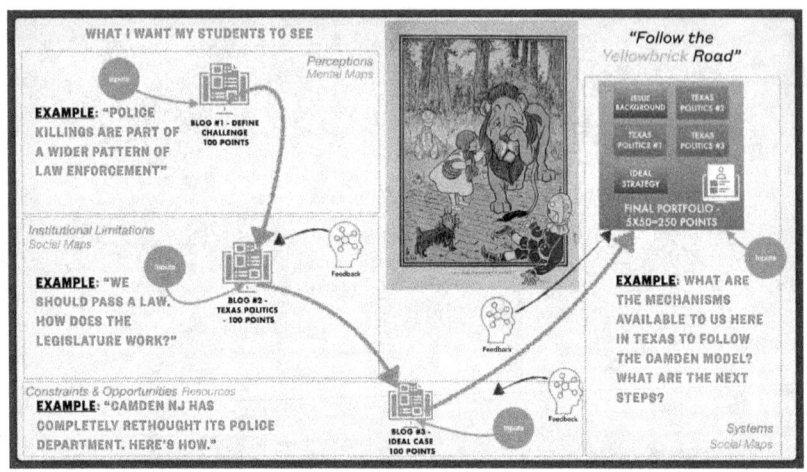

Example of an Intended Student Narrative Pathway Through My Texas Government Class

    The story of my class is also one of learning by doing. My assessments up until the final portfolio are all formative in nature. Students get credit for doing the work. The act of completing the assignment itself is demonstrating a certain learning skill. Explicitly and implicitly combining conceptual clarity, visual aids, integrated tasks, and a clear narrative pathway with waypoints along the way is central to my strategy in keeping students on track toward the final goal.

    In the *Wizard of Oz*, L. Frank Baum employed the Yellow Brick Road as a mechanism for keeping Dorothy and her friends on track through his narrative. However tangled the story became, the road was always there to lead them to their ultimate goal: the Emerald City. This is a healthy metaphor for any class. Can you see the Yellow Brick Road in your class? If you can't, don't assume your students can and don't be surprised if they get lost along the way.

Learning is the Only Lodestar

In the Covid School Wars, parents were petitioning to open in-person instruction, teachers were suing over safety concerns, college students were complaining about tuition for Zoom classes, and the disease hovered in the background like an indifferent specter. Many of these battles assumed a false absolute: online instruction is bad; in-person instruction is good. You're either in school or you're not. It therefore followed that you were either learning or not depending on whether or not you were sitting in a room with a teacher. This is silly. Leaving aside for a moment the questions of sports, vocational programs, and science labs, this was not an issue of absolutes. Learning happens everywhere and all of the time. The technologies that facilitate it are neither good nor bad. Learning just is. The physical circumstances under which it is taking place are tangential to the goal. They set the environment as we discussed in the previous chapter, but they are not determinative. We were not asked to stop making music. We were just given a different set of instruments.

As we discussed in Chapter 7, the root of the problem is that teachers do not have mastery and have often relinquished control over the tools that they have to work with. This is not entirely, or even largely, the consequence of the pandemic. It is the result of indifference to the circumstances under which they operate. As a result, they are handicapped in their ability to communicate with their students. As I have repeatedly emphasized, the underlying theme of this book is that all learning is conversational. As Diana Laurillard described it in her Conversational Frameworks (see Chapter 2) almost twenty years ago, these conversations occur between the teacher and the students, between the student and his or her peers, and within the mind of the student.

As teachers, we like to think that the most important of these conversations is between the student and teacher. The reality is that the most important conversation is the one that happens within the mind of the student. And yet, it is precisely these conversations that tend to be most neglected no matter what teaching modality is employed. If we fail to guide this conversation effectively, learning will not happen or it will happen haphazardly. Sometimes that's okay, but in a disconnected environment it can lead to a lot of misfires. In a classroom environment, good teachers rely on physical and mental cues to adjust the narrative to the room. This does not translate easily to remote learning.

I have an observation that I frequently repeat about the digital world: To make something digital is to make transparent all of its flaws. What we are seeing right now is the lifting of the veil that has obscured the vast majority of teaching that occurs in our classrooms on a daily basis. To those of us in the field of faculty development, this came as no great revelation. To parents suddenly having to grapple with the externalization of the messiness of the learning process, this might have come as a bit of a rude shock. Even in the relationship between the teacher and the student, the externalization and outsourcing of class learning goals onto unprepared students resulted in much misery and stress. A strong, explicit narrative might have avoided much of this.

This is not the first time that the exposure of what goes on in the typical classroom has resulted in derision, nor is it the first time that remote learning has been attempted on a vast scale using technology. That distinction belongs to the efforts of the Open University (OU), which started operations in 1969. A portion of this distributed university in the United Kingdom was broadcast via the BBC in the form of remote lectures. A decade later, a TV reviewer described the results as "heavy-going material... showing an intense teacher, lacking style and bad at conveying enthusiasm. Lecturing straight into the camera in a monotone from notes on a blackboard."[41] The Open University had access to sophisticated communications tools (courtesy of the BBC) and a process of iterative production. As a result, the production quality of their presentations improved markedly over the quarter century during which they used television as a mass distributor of information. Courses also had significant development teams, sometimes numbering almost 20 people.

Resources of this kind were clearly not available to most teachers struggling through the pandemic emergency, and most of us had to operate as lonely entrepreneurs as we redeveloped our courses. The OU, however, does offer some clear cautions about shifting from physical to digital/visual media. First of all, most teachers are not documentarians. Documentarians are professional storytellers who spend years of time and millions of dollars crafting compelling visual stories. They also have access to professional cinematographers, locations, and other resources a solitary teacher can only dream of having. Second, once an effort is immortalized in video, it is frozen in all of its flawed imperfection. More often than not, video, especially synchronous live sessions,

---

[41] Quoted in Daniel Weinbren, *The Open University: A History,* Manchester University Press, 2015, p. 136

fails to achieve its purpose of impactfully transmitting information from teacher to student even as it highlights every glitch and foible.

The first step in overcoming these flaws is to recognize their limitations and look for other tools to achieve the same purpose. Live teaching should work just as well in a videoconference space as it does in a classroom, but it doesn't. After all, teachers talk to their students all day. The reality is that most teachers improvise a lot in the classroom without even realizing it. I like to compare good teaching to jazz: good teachers realize that student conversations lie at the heart of all authentic learning and that context is essential for understanding. They work the classroom like Miles Davis to customize that context to benefit as many students as possible. They bring all of their conversational tools to bear. They reach out to stimulate those essential questions in the minds of their pupils. This is what is often lost when their efforts are translated into remote instruction.

Video regiments communication. Instead of making jazz with the students, teachers often feel like they are being forced to broadcast a complex symphony. Despite the best of intentions, what comes out the other end is more likely than not going to sound like a kazoo orchestra. What's worse is that this broadcast is being beamed directly into people's homes and not confined to the friendly quarters of a familiar classroom (and it's being recorded for infinite humorous playback). Teachers are forced into playing unfamiliar instruments, often using arrangements designed by non- teachers. Is it any wonder that the music that emerges at the other end is publicly discordant?

It does not have to be this way. Most teachers I have seen working online use the assigned video conferencing tool, often a slide deck, and perhaps a whiteboard tool. Assignments are shuffled through the misnamed Learning Management Systems (LMS) as they increasingly had been even before the pandemic. (The reason that I say that the LMS is a "misnomer" is that they are so infrequently used in the service of learning. Instead, they are more aptly named Content Management Systems because they are usually only used to shuffle content around and tend to work a lot less well as fluid, learner-centric spaces.) We discussed the LMS as a piece of software in greater detail in Chapter 7. However, even the best of them are often used as buckets for information and not storytelling devices. Partially, as a consequence, their design preferences tend to bias them toward their storage function and tend to neglect the need to establish clear narratives that operate above the functionality of the course shell.

What has come as a rude shock to many has been the extent to which students have tuned out from this approach. Those of us who have been teaching online for years recognize that once you lose the narrative/conversational connection, all other aspects of the course are bound to fail. We have learned that different instruments in our arsenal have to be employed to take the place of the conversations that happened around a table in a classroom. No set of online tools is perfect in replicating the in-class experience, but that's not really the point. That's like asking television to replicate the theater or concert experience. There's a reason we still have live events (at least I hope we do when you are reading this book). However, recorded events do have their upsides.

You can make a sandwich and come back to them without missing anything, for instance. The same thing is true with the canned parts of your class, which can include most, if not all, of your content.

The key is that we must learn the strengths and weaknesses of the tools we are deploying in connecting with our students. We must boil down the conversations and work from an arsenal focusing on short, curated blocks of information that advance carefully-selected elements of the course narrative, discarding everything else into the "Interested? Read More Here" category. This requires a brutal look at just how much of the content transmission part of our classes really creates deep learning (not much, unfortunately). Finally, I have recognized the precious nature of synchronous time with our students (and its stark limitations). I focus my in-person time almost exclusively on looking at their work, helping them construct their internal conversations to complete active learning assignments. The Open University had this modality built into it from the beginning through a network of tutors who met with students in vast, distributed courses and actively worked through the material with them. My synchronous sessions are explicitly designed to replicate the tutorial experience. This human element lets your students know they aren't alone as they navigate their way through your digital narratives.

COVID-19 will change education forever. It has exposed the cracks in how we deliver instruction. Thousands of videos are circulating from students that are at least as humorous as the initial OU efforts in the 70s. Some teachers have used the circumstances as a license for creativity, however, and explored the limits and modalities of their teaching. In both instances, we will have a rich mine of pretty obvious examples of what works and what doesn't.

Nothing makes me as self-critical as watching a video of myself. At the same time, I am seeing some things that actually work online *better* than they do in person. I have now built up an arsenal of tools in my classes online that I will continue to use even when I return to a more traditional classroom. This includes short videos on key subjects in the class, curated content, and examples of how to do the required assignments that are much more fleshed out than they were in previous iterations of my class. In the meantime, my online course can be taught with any amount of synchronous interactions, both online or in-person as circumstances dictate. That's because all of my synchronous time is squarely focused on the needs of the students and helping him or her navigate the intellectual puzzles my class offers for them. Each tool is targeted at its intended purpose, and all are focused squarely on the service of the learning process. The only pieces left are the imaginations of the students themselves.

Chapter 9

Designing Communities in a Digital World

While we have spent a lot of time focusing on the individual in this book, the individual only exists within a community of learning. Paradoxically, bringing students together in times of enforced (or voluntary) separation is critical to learning outcomes. This is fundamentally the function of schools. They are communities of learning. However, like in many experiences being reshaped by the digital age and brought home by the experiences of the pandemic, this is under threat. One of the primary reasons that online education has seemingly hit a wall over the last decade is that insufficient systemic attention has been brought to the problem of developing durable communities of practice, either because the software gets in the way of it or that community is in direct competition with on-campus communities. Rigid systemic practices have also significantly undermined our ability to teach and learn this way. Flexible course design runs up against the artificial dichotomy of "online" vs. "in-person." Even hybrid suffers from this as it has generally been viewed as a mechanism for increasing capacity first and reshaping learning practice only secondarily.

There are many opportunities created by digital learning. In a sense, this strategy of creating communities of learning pulls together all of the elements of the other eight. It leverages tools to empower students. It seeks to increase conversations around the individual student. It raises conversations above individual classes. Healthy communities grasp at resources, make efficient use of time and space, and transcend the bounds of individual courses. Friends persist across courses, and familiarity with fellow travelers can make unfamiliar intellectual territory seem more approachable. The atomization of instruction during the pandemic demonstrated, in stark terms, just how industrial education has alienated many students from the joys of learning. It's no accident that when schools reopened, the COVID-19 outbreaks didn't occur in the library or computer labs. They occurred in the athletic department and, most commonly, at frat houses. That's because that's where the students find their community.

The most effective approaches to developing communities of learning occur at the systemic level and, as teachers, we should advocate for the creation of systemic approaches to community-building wherever possible. These may include interdisciplinary programs, informal areas (both online and in-person), and creative approaches to scheduling courses such as short semesters, block scheduling, and other strategies that put courses into their larger learning context.

However, even on the individual instructor level digital provides some opportunities to bend time and space. As discussed in Chapter 6, we can individualize the learning experience and help students find fellow travelers by taking advantage of the fact that we are not limited by traditional time and space considerations. During Covid Summer, when I was dealing with a lot of students who had never taken a fully online course before, I took my relatively large pool of students and divided them based on their interests. With the size of the pool (64 students), these groups numbered 12-15 students each. Groups of students were encouraged to work together using a set of communication tools specifically assembled for them in my online course shell.

Reimagine your courses as groups of students rather than administrative conveniences. Take advantage of this reframing to manage individualized interactions with students. Even with groups, I was spending more time in synchronous discussion than my students were. Their experience was different from mine. While I was spending the "usual" amount of time interacting with students, their experience of synchronous interaction amounted to approximately 50% of what they would have spent sitting in class. This time, however, was enormously more productive for them because a lot less of it was spent with the usual repetitive information exchange that occurs so much in live sessions. Instead, much of that information was permanently added to the class in various places. Using frequent, persistent online announcements for semi-weekly updates of where they should be is far more productive than a set of announcements at the beginning of a class session. Half of the students miss them because they show up late and, of the remainder, only half of those are likely to have been paying attention. I can take that off of the deck from the very beginning. Instead, the entirety of my focus in these circumstances was focused on individualized attention and community-building efforts. When in-person interactions are again possible, this will still be my focus for synchronous time with my students and, most importantly, within their own community of learning.

1) Create groups to support the learning experience, not the class.
2) Lead group meetings without dominating them; encourage independent follow-up.
3) Create a sense of fellowship in the face of adversity.
4) Use technology in the service of community.
5) Advocate for systemic strategies that prioritize learning and leverage technology over bureaucratic legacies.
6) Think carefully about group size beyond the pandemic.

Planning for Antifragile Learning

As I discussed in the Introduction, in the Spring of 2020, my friend and futurist Bryan Alexander posited three scenarios for the coming years of higher education: The Post-Pandemic Campus, Covid Fall, and Toggle Term.[42] In the first scenario, the disruptions of Spring 2020 rapidly faded into the past with only minor disruptions to future activities. The Post-Pandemic campus clearly did not happen in Fall 2020. Covid Fall presented a doomsday scenario where both the responses of our institutions and the spread of virus remain beyond control. There are some that argue the jury is still out on that one. The third scenario posited oscillations of viral activity with COVID-19 reappearing spasmodically in time and place and institutions having to react in various ways in response to outbreaks. As I write this in early September 2020, Toggle Term is exactly what is taking place.

With my focus on trying to use technology to try to facilitate communities of learning, Alexander's challenge immediately got me thinking about how we create systems of learning that are resistant to the kinds of shocks imagined in his scenarios. Our priority should have been preserving learning over protecting institutions, and practices, that were already being challenged before the pandemic. This, by and large, did not happen. This was a missed opportunity, and much of student dissatisfaction centered on diminished learning experiences as a consequence. Structures should follow learning, not the other way around.

---

[42] https://bryanalexander.org/future-of-education/higher-education-in-fall-2020-three-pandemic-scenarios/

I had been working on structurally reshaping practices before the pandemic hit. After my work on the West Houston Institute, I was brought into a team working on designing a new community college campus. The problem (not at all uncommon in my experience in working on developing new campuses) was that the expectation, particularly when measured in enrollment, was that the budget allocated for the building did not allow for sufficient capacity in terms of raw square footage. I was tasked with thinking about how a campus where half the students were not physically present at any given time would look. I quickly recognized that the logic of space in a "hybrid" campus was going to be fundamentally shifted from one where space allocation was based on the formula of shuffling students from one fixed location to another to spaces that emphasized organic collaboration and the community aspects of a campus. This exploration led me to question the nature of time and space in such an environment. The strategy that emerged called for a solution that maximized the efficiency of physical spaces using the opportunities of Digital Age teaching and learning. The STAC Model described in Chapter 4 was a direct result of these efforts.

As I considered the pandemic's challenges of social distancing and unpredictable stretches of "remote teaching," it quickly occurred to me that the strategies I had developed to maximize the use of physical spaces in a Hybrid Campus could be flipped on their head and used to plan for a world in which access to existing campuses was limited by the crisis. Instead of figuring out how to pack more "headcount" into shared physical learning spaces, the goal would be to stretch existing spaces around maintaining existing headcount at much lower densities. They are essentially the same problem.

It's only logical that hybrid approaches to learning will form the core of the "new and better normal" of education in the future. This was already going to happen, but the pandemic accelerated the urgency of creating systems to meet its challenges. The Hybrid Plus strategy I am about to describe was conceived as a simple approach to designing systems of learning for the current contingency, and also as a pathway to shaping what education will look like in 5-10 years. Scarce resources at all levels of education are going to drive this trend long after the pandemic is a fading memory.

The genesis of Hybrid Plus was my work on *Discovering Digital Humanity*, which imagines new ways to augment our capabilities through strategic use of technologies. The core of that argument is that we need to reconfigure our relationship with technology, which has become increasingly dysfunctional over the last 30-40 years. Instead of being enslaved to technological processes where the few hold the power, we need to return to the vision of early technology pioneers, particularly the work of Douglas Engelbart, who saw technology as a way of "augmenting human intellect" first and foremost. Technology should make us better, not limit our choices.[43]

To do this, we need to shape technology around fundamental needs; digital technology, as I have suggested throughout this book, gives us unprecedented capacity to do this. Factories were necessary in the Industrial Age due to the nature of technology there. This is no longer the case. Most of us produce ideas, not cars

---

[43] https://www.dougengelbart.org/content/view/138

(the robots do that) in any case, and the tools we have at our disposal are a quantum leap over the teletypes, typewriters, and telephones of even 40-50 years ago. However, our practices have not kept up with these new realities, and this has led to many distortions of technology and its frequent use as a constraint rather than grasping at opportunities. Hybrid Plus is designed to grasp at those opportunities in the sphere of educational practice.

The idea of augmentation rather than constraint led me to develop a user-driven toolset analysis (the Teaching Toolset Triangle described in Chapter 1) as a first step toward understanding what kinds of tools would be necessary for the creation of "hybrid" campuses. This was, from the outset, designed to be a universal set of tools, applicable to any learning context. The onset of the pandemic suddenly required the application of these very same strategies because we were suddenly forced to explore the limits of connectivity, software, and learning practice under very ad hoc and adverse circumstances. However, many aspects of those circumstances will continue to be relevant well into the future as resources are stretched. Furthermore, the need to reach out to a much more diverse student body increases these imperatives. Demands to more effectively apply emerging technologies to achieve these challenges will only multiply. These are systemic challenges that aren't going away, and have only been highlighted by the onslaught of the pandemic.

These challenges are not really technological in nature. Understanding how technology complements our efforts is a necessary first step. However, there are systemic opportunities that must be grasped, and these will be far more challenging for many institutions than the selection of tools for our classrooms. This is because our instructional choices as teachers are bound within a system of constraints ranging from institutional and disciplinary requirements to student expectations.[44] These systemic constraints have, by and large, not changed. Meeting them, however, became exponentially harder during the pandemic. Already, in Spring 2020, **students were refusing to pay the high cost of education for what they saw as a diminished experience.**[45] Faculty were struggling to make sense of the realities of the new teaching environments they saw themselves constrained by. Above this hung the ominous question of whether it was even possible to meet these often-contradictory forces in a pandemic environment.

The answer to this was clearly "yes," but, in order to get there, we were going to have to do a root-and-branch deconstruction. This inevitably will lead to a deep analysis of how we envisioned instructional modules and the toolsets that we used to execute them. And we were going to have to do this under extreme time pressures. Some institutions aggressively pursued these kinds of challenges, but most did not, relying instead on the hope for the Post-Pandemic Campus scenario envisioned under Bryan Alexander's schema. Other institutions pursued approaches such as Brian Beatty's "HyFlex" Strategy without delving into the complex human learning interventions that this approach required for successful student outcomes.[46]

---

[44] https://www.ecampusnews.com/2019/01/29/the-biggest-barrier-to-deconstructing-education-is-not-money/

[45] https://www.insidehighered.com/news/2020/04/13/students-say-online-classes-arent-what-they-paid

[46] Beatty, Brian J. ed., Hybrid Flexible Course Design at https://edtechbooks.org/hyflex and Gannon, Kevin, "Our HyFlex

There were a variety of other approaches attempted. For instance, some institutions implemented shorter classes of either four- or five-week duration to make schedules nimbler. We are now seeing whether or not this was a good strategy for those institutions that made that level of adjustment. There is a lot of logic to this approach. It has been shown to benefit student success for *precisely the reason it works for pandemic response:* It creates lower-stakes scenarios in the face of unexpected crises. As Matt Reed, Vice President of Academic Affairs at Brookdale Community College in New Jersey noted in a recent discussion, crises happen all the time in our students' lives. The pandemic is not unique in that regard. If you are taking fewer classes over a shorter period of time, it stands to reason that fewer classes will be impacted, for shorter periods of time, in the face of any type of crisis. By definition, this makes them more resilient. Reed cited the example of Odessa College, which improved student outcomes by shortening academic terms.[47]

This kind of approach is likely to benefit learning and student success in any kind of Hybrid Plus scenario, as communities can be formed between a couple of classes. At Reed's college, students take two classes every seven weeks. This could be further exploited in a hybrid environment as those two classes could be paired across disciplines for an intense learning experience where a relatively small group of students went through the process together. Beloit College implemented this kind of

---

Experiment: What's Worked and What Hasn't," The Chronicle of Higher Education, October 26, 2020 at https://www.chronicle.com/article/our-hyflex-experiment-whats-worked-and-what-hasnt
[47] https://youtu.be/zP1hjD6GjgE

modular scheduling as part of their response to the pandemic.[48]

Another systemic need is to augment a set of **antifragile** pedagogical strategies (as outlined in Chapters 2 and 4) with instructional frameworks that help set student expectations. Nicholas Taleb describes "antifragile" as, "beyond resilience or robustness. The resilient resists shocks and stays the same; the antifragile gets better."[49] Hybrid, by its very adaptability and use of a wide range of technologies for learning, is intrinsically antifragile.

However, hybrid courses must be systemically supported to be truly "hybrid" and "antifragile." For instance, the institutional distinction between "in-person" and "online" is increasingly anachronistic and leads to gross oversimplifications that needlessly complicated responses to the pandemic. All courses today should have both online and, in many cases, in-person components. Instead of being arbitrarily labeled by a random technological construct, courses should be identified as having "synchronous" vs. "asynchronous" requirements. Some courses, such as workforce or science labs require significant synchronous capabilities. However, even in these instances, significant portions of the course can be placed online for foundational preparation, persistence, and review.

The most antifragile elements of learning are the conversations that occur in the learning process.

---

[48] https://beloitcollegeroundtable.com/2020/04/03/college-announces-two-class-modules-for-fall-2020-and-plans-for-covid-19-disruptions/

[49] Taleb, Nassim Nicholas. *Antifragile: Things That Gain from Disorder* (Incerto). Random House Publishing Group. Kindle Edition

Laurillard's conversational frameworks (discussed in Chapter 2), that underlie all forms of learning and internal conversations, are not easily disrupted (just misdirected). Mindful application of insights from these frameworks are particularly important to the less-skilled learners who make up a significant proportion of our undergraduate populations. Formative assessment and active learning are essential to their success and deeply impact the qualitative experience of even the most skilled learners. This is true no matter what learning modality is being practiced. However, many of Laurillard's "conversations" require a measure of synchronous instruction and its capacity for immediate feedback. Synchronous experiences are essential in adding depth to any instructional experience, no matter the skill of the learner in question.

How do we continue to create these kinds of rich, and in some cases essential, experiences? First of all, we need to stop spoon-feeding content, and focus our energies on the processes of assimilating that content. As has been a recurring theme in this book, **we need to consider every aspect of our classes as a set of tools** that support both synchronous and asynchronous learning. Most content can be delivered asynchronously in various forms. Applying, analyzing, and putting into practice that content however, may, in many cases require some form of synchronous interaction between the student and teacher (including librarians, mentors, counselors, tutors, and other support personnel) or between the student and his or her peers in order to achieve meaningful learning experiences.

One of the effects of the pandemic was to drastically limit the size of gatherings. Serendipitously, meaningful interactions are more likely to occur in small groups rather than in 500-person lecture halls. One strategy would therefore be to assemble a group of tools that would allow institutions to carry out in-person, synchronous instruction in groups of no more than about a dozen people complemented by online delivery of content. Smaller groups also have the beneficial side-effect of reducing pressure on physical facilities and creating opportunities for both active and informal learning to occur more easily. Hybrid toolsets can be used to stretch the capacities of physical facilities operating at vastly reduced capacity or they can be used to maximize social interactions in environments where most of the "class" is taking place online. It also is far easier to develop **communities of practice** that are closely associated with accelerating learning processes.[50] Having this kind of community will make the learning experience far more antifragile if the course is suddenly moved online.

This does not end with the pandemic. Students, particularly those living under less privileged circumstances, are constantly dealing with disruptions to their personal lives on a scale that rival those of the pandemic including illness, loss/change of job circumstances, loss of transportation, etc.; small, nimble communities of learning can cushion these kinds of shocks to their learning experience. Just because we go back to "normal" doesn't mean that our students do. These may be different kinds of shocks, but the effect is the same: they disrupt the learning process. In this way, as has also been a recurring argument in this book, the pandemic, tragic as

---

[50] https://infed.org/mobi/jean-lave-etienne-wenger-and-communities-of-practice/

it is, can provide us with useful reflections on what has been occurring all along.

Nimbleness is in large part conditioned by size. With proper planning and support, learning in smaller chunks, coupled with creating meaningful communities of practice, will cushion the effects of periodic shocks to our physical environments. At the same time, it will likely increase the meaningfulness of the experience. It's time to double down on quality, not give up on it. If there is one thing this pandemic has taught us, it is that those communities with stores of human and social capital have proven to be the most resilient. Now is the time for us to look at what makes learning most human and build our educational communities round them. We must never forget that we are in the business of building humans. Hybrid Plus is designed with those assumptions in mind.

The Hybrid Plus Model

What has struck me about most systemic responses to the pandemic was the poor understanding that most educational systems have about the fundamentals of their businesses. This book is an effort to tie together nine strands of thinking about the relationship between teaching and technology, and to boil them down to their essential connective tissue. In a recent survey, 75% of students expressed dissatisfaction with the experiments undertaken in Spring 2020 collectively and aptly entitled "remote learning."[51] The students in this survey found the remote learning experience unsurprisingly isolating and unsatisfying. The learning outcomes of the experience are

---

[51] https://oneclass.com/blog/featured/177356-7525-of-college-students-unhappy-with-quality-of-elearning-during-covid-19.en.html

also likely to be problematic, as early indicators seem to be showing.[52] The experience was a frustrating one for many instructors and students, for entirely predictable reasons. We did the best we could. However, any good designer will tell you to learn from the flaws of your experience and iterate moving forward.

Hybrid Plus is a holistic approach to teaching and learning that is designed specifically to address the problems of student connectedness coupled with the uncertainties of an environment characterized by the pandemic. At the same time, it recognizes that there are real administrative challenges involved in facing a "toggle term" effectively. The strategy has three elements (all based on elements discussed in greater detail elsewhere in the book):

I. *Create Student-Centered Instruction (Chapters 2, 3, 5, 6)* – Faculty must thoroughly self-assess their classes and ask themselves the following questions:
    1. Which parts of instruction are best achieved asynchronously?
    2. How can I maximize the impact of limited synchronous interactions with my students?
    3. How can I structure assessments to be more authentic and meaningful and away from turning assessment into a game?

---

[52] https://www.dese.gov.au/system/files/doc/other/lamb_-_impact_of_learning_from_home.pdf

II. *Tailor toolsets (Chapters 1, 4, 7)* – Maximize the impact of connectivity with our students. We need to assess the tools available to faculty and students with an eye toward facilitating teaching and learning. The goal here is to identify and rectify deficiencies before the semester starts. Some key commonalities that should always be observed in this environment are:

1. Technical barriers of all types must be minimized to the greatest extent possible. For instance, videoconferencing systems should be lightweight, system agnostic, have a dial-in option, and work robustly on mobile devices. Access to technology should not limit access to learning to the greatest extent possible.

2. Whenever possible, technology should prioritize student-driven functionality over other concerns. For instance, one of the issues that many students face is how to engage in informal learning with other students. Informal learning is critical to student success. Students should be encouraged to use, and be provided with, synchronous platforms for meeting with other students. One of the biggest victims of isolation from campuses is isolation from other students outside of class. A student-driven video conferencing solution, coupled

with an asynchronous, student-driven, chat and meetup functionality, is key to developing communities of practice among students.

III. *Create flexible scheduling systems (Chapters 5, 6, 8)* – Physical environments should provide as much in-person, human interaction as circumstances permit. We should create flexible scheduling arrangements that allow teachers and students to come together on an ad hoc basis to complement their online experiences. Whether we are dealing with CDC guidelines or the needs of online/hybrid students, these groups require flexible arrangements in time as well as to accommodate varying sizes of groups. The importance of this kind of human contact should not be underestimated. The challenge for administrators is to create the kind of flexible scheduling system and to communicate the availability of different kinds of facilities to faculty on an as-needed basis. This is a particularly important element to those courses requiring hands-on instruction, such as many workforce programs, as well as any academic courses requiring labs for experimentation. Attention to support services that would benefit from a physical presence should also be given.

Planning around these three elements will give institutions and the students which they serve maximum flexibility in meeting unexpected circumstances, while preserving the integrity of the teaching and learning process and, most importantly, engaging students to the greatest extent possible. If the pandemic has taught us anything, it is that we can no longer afford to treat students like widgets being processed through the systems of learning. COVID-19 has blown apart the factory walls and the parts have been scattered to the wind. We need to think carefully about how we put them back together again.

Technology can provide a key linkage to building a new kind of learning environment. However, learning for many students will be crippled if those technological solutions are not paired with systemic adaptations. Teachers must adapt their systems of engagement with the communities of learning that they are responsible for. Students must be encouraged to adapt their systems of interaction with each other as well as their learning (learning to learn is part of any learning process). Institutions must facilitate constructive engagement at all levels and must therefore adapt institutional practices around maximizing systems of interaction in an environment without walls. We may have to let go of some already outdated systems to achieve that. However, the pandemic may provide a catalyst for an overdue reimagining of our learning ecosystems. There is great opportunity for innovation here.

Final Thoughts:
Teaching is Evergreen

Since the first humans taught each other how to hunt and survive, we have been teaching each other. It is only within the last 150 years that we have industrialized teaching and made it more vulnerable to outside shocks. While not many would have predicted the impact of the pandemic on our mechanisms of teaching, it was becoming abundantly clear long before 2020 that automation would begin to have a similar effect.

What has become increasingly evident to me as I have researched, written, and applied technology over the last decade is that our struggles to adapt to new circumstances lie not within our inability to facilitate learning but rather within the systems that have grown up to scale it. Teachers know that the most important interactions in learning happen between teacher and student; nothing will ever change that.

If the pandemic has taught us anything, it's that good teaching is the difference-maker under adverse circumstances. Many have risen to embrace the challenges of remote teaching: If you are holding this book, I can safely assume you are one of them. However, everything in this book is a product of work that happened long before the first victims of the disease fell ill. The reason that I felt I could write this book was not because I considered myself to be some great seer, but, rather, my recognition of two facts: First, *all* teaching is done under adverse circumstances. We have papered that fact over with routine, but we should never mistake the routine for learning. Second, that we have been granted vast new arrays of tools to attack the wicked problem of learning. We just have to adjust our mindsets around possibility and learn to design for the unexpected. Learning is always a little bit unexpected.

Leadership's job is to facilitate learning. Full stop. That learning occurs at the most human of levels. Therefore, leadership needs to prioritize that relationship and build all else around it. It also needs to recognize that the best thing it can do, most of the time, is to set the conditions where small changes can be made, get out of the way, and figure out how to share and scale it.

That is not the part under threat today. If anything, the parts under threat are those that serve to isolate us from our students, such as massive lecture classes that offer very little benefit synchronously or standardized testing regimes that dehumanize the student in the name of conformity to a meaningless norm. For decades now, it has been the humanity of the teacher-student relationship that has overcome these systemic obstacles. None of this is new or was brought on by the pandemic.

That human connection is what has saved my classes even as all other parts of them have come under the intense strain of "remote" learning. One of my proudest achievements during Covid Spring was the fact that I only lost one of my group of vulnerable students due to the dislocations of moving online in mid-semester. This was in large part due to my aggressive outreach efforts and flexibility in keeping my students engaged. I was able to do this while maintaining the standards and goals laid out in my syllabus at the outset of the semester. I credit this success to making deft use of the tools available to me; working closely with my students on learning how to learn early on in the semester when we were still face-to-face; and taking advantage of digital opportunities when class suddenly went online. These opportunities included merging synchronous meetings to focus on group projects and assessment of their work as well as scheduling individual videoconferencing meetings with every one of the students in the class to gauge their learning needs in the new environment. This was actually facilitated by my not being beholden to physical space and time as I could meet with a student any time both of us had the time.

 My observation that "to make something digital is to make transparent all of its flaws" has not been flattering to many of the systems we take for granted as teachers. I think we all realized at some level that the way most of us assessed our students was flawed. The long, hard look at cheating in the online world has forced many to accept that the problem lies not so much in our students but, rather, in the meaninglessness of the regimen of testing in which they find themselves trapped. Like all technologies, tests aren't bad. It's the way we use them that is. Going digital exposed that reality to the light of day in stark terms. That doesn't mean going digital is bad. It means the underlying testing structure is what's rotten. Education will be stronger for the light.

During the pandemic, we all experienced the phenomenon of the "stopped clock." Confined to our homes day after day, time seemed to move in stops and start. Panic seemed to offer little outlet. Instead, the crisis provoked many of us into reflection. That is the genesis of much of the work in this book.

Crisis is often a moment of opportunity. It is a moment for teaching. It provides a moment to teach the world what real teaching looks like. It provides a moment to teach our systems of education what they can be. Most importantly, it provides a moment for us to teach ourselves. I have always been excited about grasping a future where technology allowed me to break from a present where my work with students constantly threatened to become repetitive, boring, and, most depressingly, ineffective. The pandemic pushed me to try many new things that I had considered but never fully implemented. It made me apply work on everything from systems thinking to storytelling to assessment practices in whole new ways. It forced me to teach myself.

If we demand that technology facilitate the human and not the system, then the pandemic's challenge to education will result in stronger, potentially antifragile, systems of learning. If not, we will continue to struggle with the realities of an increasingly anachronistic educational environment. We can and must take advantage of digital transparency to explore the strengths and weaknesses of everything we do as teachers. This will show us opportunities to open pathways that preserve the fundamental human relationships. These relationships, in turn, form the core of teaching and learning, and it is only by prioritizing them that we can begin to discard the commodification of education developed during the

Industrial Age. The pandemic will end, but our automated future is inevitable. The pathways we chart in getting there, however, will profoundly shape the course of teaching and learning for generations to come. Even before the pandemic, we were living in an inflection point. The pandemic merely stressed the system to make that point clear. If we take advantage of this opportunity to choose wisely, we can take advantage of the array of digital opportunities within our grasp and get back to the ancient mission of teaching: to build better humans.

Bibliography

Further Reading -

Articles:
- Designing Learning Environments Based on a Learner-Centric Model for Physical, Hybrid, and Online Learning: A Preliminary Exploration.
  http://www.ideaspaces.net/learner-centric-model/
- The STAC Model: Rethinking the Basic Functionality of Informal Learning Spaces; *Current Issues in Education (forthcoming) Current Issues in Education*, 21(2). Retrieved from https://cie.asu.edu/ojs/index.php/cieatasu/article/view/1915
- Thinking Backward: A Knowledge Network for the Next Century; Current Issues in Education (forthcoming)
  http://www.ideaspaces.net/thinking-backward/

Blogs:
- Scolus Interruptus: Making Systems of Learning Antifragile, *eCampus News*, May 13, 2020
  https://www.ecampusnews.com/2020/05/13/scholus-interruptus-making-systems-of-learning-antifragile/
- Listening and Learning in an Era of Social Distancing, March 22, 2020
  http://www.ideaspaces.net/listening-and-learning-in-an-era-of-social-distancing/
- Designing Instructional Systems in a Time of Crisis, March 19, 2020
  http://www.ideaspaces.net/designing-instructional-systems-in-a-time-of-crisis/
- Rethinking Tools for Hybrid and Online Learning; *eCampus News*, February 28, 2020.
  https://www.ecampusnews.com/2020/02/28/rethinking-tools-for-hybrid-and-online-learning/
- Three Strategies to Start Reimagining the Learning Management System, *eCampus News*, April 11, 2019.
  https://www.ecampusnews.com/2019/04/11/reimagining-learning-management-system/

Key Sources:

- Conway, Mel, "How Do Committees Invent," *Datamation* (April 1968), pp. 28-31 http://www.melconway.com/Home/pdf/committees.pdf
- Laurillard, Diana, *Rethinking University Teaching: A Framework for the Effective Use of Learning Technologies* (London: Routledge, 2002).
- Laurillard, Diana, "Pedagogical forms for mobile learning: framing research questions" (2007) http://discovery.ucl.ac.uk/10000627/1/Mobile_C6_Laurillard.pdf
- Laurillard, Diana, "The Pedagogical Challenges to Collaborative Technologies," *Computer Supported Collaborative Learning* (4/2009), pp. 4-20.
- Lave, Jean and Etienne Wenger, *Situated Learning: Legitimate Peripheral Participation* (Cambridge: Cambridge University Press, 1991).
- Muller, Michael J. and Allison Druin, "Participatory Design: The Third Space in HCI," in Julie A. Jacko and Andrew Sears eds., *The Human-Computer Interaction Handbook: Fundamentals, Evolving Technologies and Emerging Applications* (Hillsdale, NJ: L. Erlbaum Associates, 2003), pp. 1051-1068
- Papert, Seymour and Idit Harel, "Situating Constructionism" in Papert and Harel eds., *Constructionism* (New York: Praeger, 1991)
- Papert, Seymour, *Mindstorms* (New York: Basic Books, 1980, 1993)

- Protopsaltis, Spiros and Sandy Baum, "Does Online Education Live Up to Its Promise: A Look at the Evidence and Implications for Federal Policy," http://mason.gmu.edu/~sprotops/OnlineEd.pdf

Acknowledgements

As is always the case, there are numerous threads that came together to make this book possible. However, my ongoing conversations with Drs. Ruben Puentedura and Bryan Alexander were decisive in shaping many of the pieces that make up this book. They constantly open doors to approaches and theories that I can then synthesize into practical applications for both myself and my various audiences. They have also read many of the chapters and given me valuable feedback. Any flaws in the synthesis of those ideas, however, are entirely my responsibility.

I would also like to thank Dr. Zachary Hodges, president of Houston Community College Northwest, for launching me on a number of key paths in rethinking the interaction between physical and digital spaces in hybrid learning as well as giving me the opportunity to assist him and his team in the development of a campus model designed for hybrid education. This work led directly to the ideas of the STAC Model, the Teaching Toolset Triangle, and Hybrid Plus.

Mark Tiller and Dr. "Butch" Herod have also served as sounding boards throughout my teaching career and they both contributed practical insights to much of the work here. Working with Dr. Herod and the West Houston Institute team in developing the Learning Spaces Initiative at the Institute allowed me to develop a number of crucial connections. Thanks to Jordan Carswell, Alexandra Almestica, Susan Thompson, and Dr. Laura Williamson in helping me brainstorm and workshop a number of key ideas along the way.

And I want to thank those who took their time to read a final draft of this book under a very tight schedule, Paul Signorelli, John Hildreth, and Danielle Haymes. Particular thanks go to Paul, who spent a large number of hours inserting comma splices into the work. Their unique insights and eagle eyes helped with its final polish.

The ShapingEDU Team at Arizona State University has been a key partner and support over the last few years. Particular thanks go to Dr. Lev Gonick, Samantha Becker, and Laura Geringer for providing key linkages to a network of "dreamers and doers" who have served as key inspirations and sounding boards. Special thanks go to my fellow storytellers Paul Signorelli and Karina Branson for keeping me on the straight and narrow.

Finally, and most importantly, I have to thank my family for their tireless patience and support as I have seen my life disrupted by jobs and pandemics. My parents, Ed and Wini, are a source of inspiration and constant support. But a special thanks goes to my patient wife, Lorie, and our wonderful children, who put up with my constant bouts of frustrating writer's block. I would not be here but for them.

About the Author

Tom Haymes has almost 40 years of technology experience culminating in his role as director of the design team for the West Houston Institute, an integrated innovation center for Houston Community College. He has been a Technology Director for a college of 20,000 students, a teacher, managed innovation teams across a wide range of projects, and has developed a series of strategies around technology adoption and integration. He has published articles on a number of topics ranging from technology adoption to military history. He was formerly a contributing editor to the New Media Consortium and served on the board of their futuring project, *The Horizon Report*. He is currently a Storyteller in Residence and Mayor of the Humanizing Education Neighborhood for Arizona State University's ShapingEDU Project. He maintains a consulting business at ideaspaces.net where he consults on Technology Assessment (Teaching Toolset Triangle), Space Design (ELITE Strategy), Professional Development, Hybrid Educational Design (Hybrid Plus), Digital Communications Strategies, Organizational Design, and Digital Futuring.

www.ingramcontent.com/pod-product-compliance
Lightning Source LLC
Chambersburg PA
CBHW070058080526
44586CB00013B/1108